By Harry L. Shapiro

Peking Man
The Heritage of the Bounty
(now *The Pitcairn Islanders*)
Aspects of Culture
Race Mixture
The Jewish People
Man, Culture and Society (editor)

PEKING MAN

HARRY L. SHAPIRO

SIMON AND SCHUSTER | NEW YORK

Copyright © 1974 by Harry L. Shapiro
All rights reserved
including the right of reproduction
in whole or in part in any form
Published by Simon and Schuster
Rockefeller Center, 630 Fifth Avenue
New York, New York 10020
Designed by Edith Fowler
Manufactured in the United States of America

1   2   3   4   5   6   7   8   9   10

Library of Congress Cataloging in Publication Data

Shapiro, Harry Lionel
Peking man.
Includes index.
1.   Sinanthropus pekinensis.   I.   Title.
GN284.7.S48   1975   573'.3   74-19396
ISBN 0-671-21899-9

To
H. J. T. V.

CONTENTS

PREFACE

My good friend Michael Korda is responsible for my writing this book. It was his enthusiastic urging that prompted me, somewhat reluctantly, to undertake the task. And I am now deeply grateful to him for the unexpected satisfaction I have had in assembling this story of Peking man.

My initial reluctance arose from the fact that I had no new solution nor even an anticlimactic denouement to offer for the mystery of the loss of the fossil remains of Peking man. It was thirty years after their disappearance that they again became front page news, and once again a series of strange developments took place as a result. These, and new information on the events leading up to the loss, finally seemed important enough to relate as best I could if only for the record. There was also, of course, the inherent drama that offered an interest of its own.

In presenting this story, I have also attempted to reconstruct something of the life, manners and appearance of these precursors of ours, who lived so far back in our past that they had been completely forgotten. What we recover can only be by inference, but inference based on reliable knowledge and used with discretion can be extremely useful. Mine I hope conforms to these requirements.

1

PEKING MAN DISAPPEARS

For over half a million years, Peking man had lain buried and unknown in a limestone hill in Chou Kou Tien, near Peking. When his existence was first announced in 1926, the news came as a bombshell to the scientific world, for no relics of primitive man this far back had ever been found in China, or indeed anywhere else on the mainland of Asia. And in 1941, fifteen years later, his precious remains were gone: stolen, lost or destroyed, no one knew. Never in the history of the recovery of the fossil record of human evolution had there been a disaster of such magnitude, for these ancient bones represented a veritable population of at least forty individuals—men, women and children—from a stage of human evolution previously unknown.

At first the loss seemed incredible because, since the publication in the nineteenth century of Darwin's *Origin of Species*, fossils—as the sole tangible evidence of evolution— had taken on a kind of sanctity. They were the rare fragments of successive worlds: the keys to understanding the forms that life had taken in its tireless and unending adaptation to the environment. And among these relics, none had a more immediate interest than those that marked the course of human evolution.

The tragedy of this loss had a poignancy for students of

human evolution that was not immediately evident to the general public. One might suppose that once the fossils had been discovered, carefully studied and the findings published they would have served their purpose in contributing to the reconstruction of the past. Their loss then might be regrettable, but not necessarily irreparable. Actually, to those familiar with the history of paleontological studies, it is common knowledge that there is no end to the study of such relics. Time and again, well-known and published specimens have been reexamined, and basic reassessments of their relationships have followed from the new insights that fresh discoveries provide. This is illustrated in the history of *Ramapithecus*, one of a series of fossils brought to light in 1934 from a Miocene–Pliocene level in the Siwalik hills of India. G. E. Lewis, who reported its discovery, placed it in an apelike category known as *Dryopithecus*, where it remained for many years, its true significance unappreciated. Then in the 1960's, Elwyn Simons, a Yale paleontologist, began an intensive restudy of the *Dryopithecines*. On the basis of the much more sophisticated knowledge of primate evolution that had by then developed, he was able to demonstrate to the satisfaction of many experts that *Ramapithecus*, far from being an ape, was actually close to the line leading to the family of hominids that includes man. Indeed, because of the spottiness of the fossil record, new discoveries often enforce a reexamination of previous, often tentative, reconstructions. Under such circumstances, casts may sometimes serve for an original specimen, but they are never as good.

For these reasons, the institutions that house collections of fossils regard them as invaluable for continuing research, and those institutions that are lucky enough to own any important fossils protect them with special care. Restrictions are apt to be more stringent for human fossils than for others, with permission to handle and examine them usually granted only to qualified students.

The Peking fossils were at the time of their disappearance the only representatives of this stage of human evolution. No others existed. If one of the scores of scattered Neanderthal relics had been destroyed or lost, though most regrettable, it would not have meant that the type was no longer available for scientific study and research. Although each specimen as a variant of its type is important, the others can, to a considerable extent, provide adequate information. But with the loss of all representatives of a specific stage of evolution, the situation becomes quite different.

Although a few additional representatives of this ancient population have recently been discovered as a result of renewed exploration by the Chinese, it is unlikely that anything approaching the original sample will ever be restored.

It is a rare thing to have an array of fossils representing a series of individuals from a single population. It provides a knowledge of the variation and range of the type that is invaluable in assessing its position. All too often a single specimen is all we have to illustrate a particular development in evolution.

Professor Franz Weidenreich was the scientist charged with the responsibility of studying the fossils of Peking man and publishing his results and conclusions. In 1934 he had been chosen by the China Medical Board of the Rockefeller Foundation to fill the post at the Peking Union Medical College left vacant on the death of Professor Davidson Black, who previously had been responsible for the study of the fossils at the Cenozoic Research Laboratory. Weidenreich's medical career in Germany, both as a teacher and in research, was renowned. After achieving distinction in hematology and osteology, he had become interested in fossil man and had published in 1928 an outstanding report on the Ehringsdorf skull, a Neanderthaloid fossil found in Germany. At the time of his appointment to China to continue the work on the newly discovered Peking man fossils, Weidenreich, was a visiting Professor at the University of Chicago. As a Jew, he found Nazi Germany intolerable, and the post in China offered an alternative. But I suspect it was largely his deep interest in the problems of unraveling man's evolutionary past that so strongly attracted him to Peking, for his reputation would easily have won him a distinguished post in the United States.

When Weidenreich reached Peking, active excavation at Chou Kou Tien was still under way, and new discoveries were being added to the existing evidence. These were mostly teeth, sometimes separate, sometimes imbedded in pieces of the jaws, a few long bones and, most significant, skull fragments. These had to be cleaned and the hard, stony incrustations carefully removed before they could be studied in detail. With characteristic and dedicated application, Weidenreich began within a year or so to issue a series of authoritative monographs on the fossils—the mandibles, the dentition, the brain casts and the long bones—leaving for last a monumental and wide-ranging study of the skull itself.

In 1937 fieldwork at Chou Kou Tien had ceased as a result of local tensions between the Nationalist Chinese and the Japanese invaders. An exchange of fire at the Marco Polo Bridge had finally touched off Chinese resistance. But detailed research on the anatomical structure of the fossils, though complicated by these external affairs, continued in the Cenozoic Research Laboratory of the Geological Survey of China at the Peking Union Medical College. The immediate Japanese menace was somewhat cushioned by the fact that the P.U.M.C. was an institution founded and supported by the American Rockefeller Foundation, for at this stage of the Japanese incursion, foreign interests in China were respected. Their embassies and their military contingents were unmolested.

Yet the sense of danger and encroachment grew steadily and a considerable unease became manifest. For those in charge of the activities of the Cenozoic Research Laboratory, the safety of their precious fossils became a major issue. Long before we in the United States began seriously to anticipate any deliberate hostilities from the Japanese, the Chinese and the Americans stationed in China were becoming extremely sensitive to the increasing threat of a Japanese conflict with the United States. Under such an eventuality the laboratory could be expected to fall into Japanese hands and its contents to be confiscated.

It may seem that the officers and scientists at the Cenozoic Research Laboratory were unduly fearful. Why, one might ask, would Japanese soldiers have any interest in the old fossil bones? Would their officers be sufficiently sophisticated to know their paleontological value and to search for them in the storage vaults? Yet one of the first things the Japanese did when they declared war and took over the P.U.M.C. was to search for these fossils and to subject any staff members they could lay hands on to rigorous pressure and persistent cross-examination.

Mr. Pei Wen-chung, who had actively participated in the excavations at Chou Kou Tien and in 1929 discovered the first skull of Peking man, has described the questioning in some detail in *Studies in Chinese Prehistory*. He was cross-examined not only by Japanese anthropologists but also by official government agents. He also mentions that Mr. Trevor Bowen, the American administrator for the P.U.M.C., was subjected to five difficult days of interrogation.

This passion of the Japanese for fossil collections is reflected in their confiscation of an important assemblage of fossil foraminifera that Professor H. Tahlmann had collected and had stored in Java. This collection had an obvious commercial value for oil exploration in that area and could therefore have been valuable to Japanese interests. Since human fossils have no such commercial significance, I can only surmise that the unrelenting Japanese search for the Peking man fossils was either the expression of a special drive by Japanese anthropologists eager to have such an extraordinary collection for their own research purposes, or a kind of collector's passion so widespread among the Japanese. Another example of Japanese fossil-raiding concerned one of the Solo skulls that the distinguished paleontologist Ralph von Koenigswald had in his care in Java, where he had been working at the outbreak of hostilities. These fossils, eleven more or less complete crania, represented a somewhat Neanderthaloid population that had lived in Java long after the time of *Pithecanthropus* or Peking man. In addition, Von Koenigswald had found some important new examples of the early *Pithecanthropus* type. His first concern after the Japanese invasion was for the safety of the valuable and as yet unstudied specimens. As he expected, he was put into a prison camp for the duration of the war, but before he was incarcerated he took steps to safeguard the collection. On his release at the end of hostilities, he discovered that one of his Solo skulls was, despite his precautions, missing. On leaving Java in the autumn of 1945, he came directly to the American Museum of Natural History, bringing his collection of fossils—the richest array I had ever seen or handled at any one time. He was, however, like a shepherd who had brought his flock home safely except for one lost ewe lamb.

Shortly after Von Koenigswald's arrival, I received a letter from Walter Fairservis, a former student of mine and a close friend. As a young lieutenant, Fairservis had been assigned to the Military Intelligence Service in Japan, and he wrote now asking if there was anything I wished him to do for me while he was there. Somewhat in jest, I replied suggesting that he try to find Von Koenigswald's lost Solo skull. A couple of months later I received a request from Washington to provide a precise description of the skull. After consulting with Von Koenigswald, I sent the information on to Washington, feeling somewhat puzzled but also suspecting that Fairservis was on to something. Yet as I was entering the museum one morning a few days before Christmas, I was completely surprised to meet Fairservis, carrying a box containing the lost Solo skull. He had been commissioned to bring it back by hand and deliver it to Von Koenigswald, who probably had never received so welcome and unexpected a Christmas present. Fairservis had found the fossil in the Emperor's Household Museum as part of the Imperial collection of curiosities.

In retrospect, it now seems justifiable for the guardians of Peking man to have been deeply concerned about the safety of these fossils. From notes and letters that have survived and from Pei's firsthand account, it is clear that considerable discussion was going on in Peking about the steps that should be taken to insure their safety and their continued possession by the Chinese.

Why, one wonders, did Weidenreich not take the fossils with him when he left for the United States? He knew that the Cenozoic Research Laboratory at Peking Union Medical College, where the fossils were kept, had thus far escaped Japanese raiding only because it was technically under American supervision, and Japan and the United States were not yet at war. But the prospects for the relics' future safety already looked bleak. The record makes it clear that he was deeply concerned. The options open to him and the officials in charge of the Cenozoic Research Laboratory were these: They could put the fossils in a secret vault or some other hiding place in Peking, thereby avoiding the danger of shipping them out of the country in turmoil; they could dispatch them to some quieter section of China where they could be protected (Southwest China was one such area considered by the director); or they could send them out of the country altogether. Shipment to the United States was seriously contemplated. In a letter written January 10, 1941, to Dr. Henry Houghton, director of the Peking Union Medical College, Drs. W. H. Wong and T. H. Yin weighed the merits of the second and third choices. They concluded that in view of the practical difficulties of sending the fossils to the Geological Survey station in Southwest China, it might be wiser to allow Weidenreich to carry them with him to some institution in the United States, this despite an understanding with the Rockefeller Foundation that anything excavated at Chou Kou Tien must remain in China.

A letter dated July 11, 1941, from Weidenreich to Wong summarizes a great deal of discussion and correspondence on the disposition of the fossils:

> We arrived at the conclusion that it involved too great a risk to take the originals as part of my baggage. If they were discovered by the customs control in an embarkation or transit port, they could be confiscated. In addition, it had to be taken into account that the objects are too valuable to expose them to an unprotected voyage in so dangerous a time. Considering all the pros and cons we decided, at least for the moment, it would be wise to leave the originals where they are now, that is in the safe of the Cenozoic Research Laboratory in the building of the Department of Anatomy at the P.U.M.C.

He went on to say that the Rockefeller Foundation authorities in New York agreed, but that the matter could be reconsidered if conditions deteriorated further.

I remember talking with Weidenreich about it, and I recall that the decision not to risk shipping the fossils in his private baggage was made after he had failed to persuade the U.S. ambassador and the commanding officer of the Marine Corps in Peking to send them out in official U.S. baggage, thus avoiding the red tape of customs regulations.

At any rate, nothing was done during those crucial months of 1941. Weidenreich left China, taking beautifully prepared casts, photographs and detailed drawings that were essential for the completion of his study of Peking man.

In August 1941, after Weidenreich's departure, Mr. Pei relates that Mr. Wong Wen-hao, director of the Institute of Geological Survey, wrote to the American ambassador, Mr. Nelson T. Johnson, asking him to arrange for the shipment of the fossils to the United States, where they could be stored in safety for return to China after hostilities had ceased. After some unexplained delay and further pressure from Pei, a telegram arrived at the United States Embassy in Peking from Mr. Johnson, then stationed in Chungking, with instructions to proceed in the business of getting the fossils out of the country. This was sometime in mid-November 1941. Looking back, we can see that time was running out, for this was only some three weeks before war was declared by the Japanese on the United States, after which nothing could be done.

What happened next was concealed from us here in the United States. With the outbreak of war on December 8 (Chinese time), communications ceased. The American officials of the P.U.M.C. captured by the Japanese were placed under arrest, and their Chinese colleagues were unable to write even if they had had anything to tell. Pei, who was as concerned for the safety of the fossils as anyone could be, knew little about what had actually happened. As he wrote:

> We should be grateful to our American friends, who not only had assumed the entire responsibility for transporting "Peking Man", but also were prepared to shoulder the blame if they should become prisoners after the war broke out between Japan and the United States so as not to implicate Chinese (namely myself). Anyway, of our American friends, the two most important ones were Mr. Houghton, the Dean of Hsieh-ho Medical School [the Peking Union Medical College] and Mr. Bowen, the Administrator. They personally took care of the packing of the *Sinanthropus* [Peking Man] specimens as well as their transportation, without letting me participate or know. Their spirit of shouldering blame for others was indeed most admirable and something for which one has to be grateful.

In his account, Pei reports that early in the morning of December 8, when the Japanese took over the Peking Union Medical College, one of the first things they did was to open and examine the contents of the safe in the Department of Anatomy. Obviously, the fossils had a high priority and the looting must have been planned well in advance. In confirmation of this, Pei records that Professors Hasebe and Takai of the Tokyo Imperial College had arrived in Peking before hostilities broke out. That this had been arranged in order for them to seize the fossils at the first possible moment, and before they could be removed by the Chinese, is confirmed by Takai's request that he be allowed to work in the laboratory. Pei was convinced that this was intended to put Takai in a strategic position to familiarize himself with safety provisions and to watch for any Chinese maneuvers to secrete the fossils. Hasebe also, as Pei phrased it, was "plotting in the dark."

Frustrated by finding only casts in the safe, the Japanese then explored every other source of information available. Pei, of course, was exposed to persistent interrogation, was bribed with a "puppet" professorship, was appealed to on the grounds that "China and Japan belong to one family," presumably unified against the West. He was accused of being an agent for Chungking and was confined to Peking. Hasebe even invited him to collaborate in reopening the excavations at Chou Kou Tien. "Only by this time," Pei observed, "I began to understand the careful planning of our American friends, Mr. Houghton and Mr. Bowen, who had kept me from knowing anything when they carried out the packing and transportation of the *Sinanthropus* specimens."

The Japanese, however, were not easily discouraged, for Pei records that about a year and a half later, in April 1943, he was again visited by a Japanese detective with the English name "George," who informed him that he was on a mission from the Japanese Ministry of War, charged with locating the Peking man fossils. Pei declared that he later discovered that it was Hasebe who had persuaded the Japanese War Ministry to make this renewed attempt. "George" was apparently very efficient, for Pei comments on his ability in getting to everyone involved, and particularly to Mr. Bowen, who must have been a prisoner in Peking. Pei writes that Bowen, as a result of being ferreted out by George, "suffered five days of hardship from the Japanese Military Police Corps."

From this point on, Pei's account becomes somewhat contradictory, if his earlier statement of planned ignorance of the disposal of the fossils is correct. His gratitude at having been wisely kept uninformed of the packing and transportation of the fossils appears somewhat misplaced in the light of the description he gives of the role he played in these very procedures. He states that at the beginning of November 1941 (before the outbreak of war) "we did the packing in two white wooden boxes." These are described in other firsthand accounts as footlockers of the kind used by the Marines for baggage. The fossil relics of Peking man were carefully packed in cotton in smaller boxes that were fitted into the two footlockers, which were then labeled A and B. This agrees completely with the recollection of Mrs. Claire Taschdjian, who had been an assistant to Dr. Weidenreich and had remained in Peking after his departure. Pei also mentions that some *Homo sapiens* fossils—the Upper Cave skulls—were packed with the Peking relics, another loss, usually overlooked in the concern for the disappearance of the more primitive specimens.

Still another confirmation of this operation came to me recently from Miss Mary E. Ferguson, who at the time was Registrar and Secretary of the Board of Transfers of the Peking Union Medical College. She wrote: "From my office window I watched Mr. Bowen taking a locker trunk across the marble court to the front gate of the College to a car in which it went to the U.S. Marine barracks. Whether or not there was more than one locker trunk, I cannot say, but I can vouch for there having been at least one."

Pei, continuing his account, says that the two boxes he had helped pack were sent to the U.S. Embassy, from there to be transferred to the U.S. Marine Corps stationed in the Peking area. It was the Marines who were charged with their safe conduct to the United States. It is also clear from Pei's recollections that he knew that the boxes were to be shipped on the S.S. *President Harrison* along with the Marine personnel. The ship was due in Chingwangtao, the port city for Tientsin, on December 8, but she never reached the harbor. En route from Manila, she was pursued by a Japanese warship and ran aground outside the mouth of the Yangstze River.

In May 1943, about a month after George's visit and search, Pei records that word came through that Peking man, or his fossil remains, had been found at Tientsin; but this was shortly denied, and it was stated that whatever had been discovered there had nothing to do with the lost specimens. But Pei continues by saying that from this time on the Japanese made no further search for the fossils. I don't know whether this was mere coincidence or whether perhaps the Japanese had found the fossils, or some of them, at Tientsin and hence no longer needed to search for them.

Pei himself seems to have concluded that the fossils were lost. He mentions that the two footlockers had been shipped to a warehouse at Chingwangtao to await the S.S. *President Harrison*. This warehouse, he writes, was twice ransacked and plundered by Japanese soldiers, and the two boxes were "most probably destroyed by them." He then adds, "nevertheless it is also quite possible that they had hidden the boxes."

At the end of the war, when the Allied Command was in Japan, one final flare-up again raised hopes that were all too quickly dampened. On November 19, 1945, a cablegram from the Central News Agency in Tokyo was received in Peking and published in the Chinese papers. It announced that the "skeleton of Peking man previously stolen and transported to Tokyo" had been found by the Supreme Allied Command. Alas, Pei reports that what was sent back to China turned out to be plaster casts, no doubt those that had been stored at the Peking Union Medical College. After all this, Pei could only sadly conclude in 1945 that "the whereabouts of 'Peking man' are unknown."

While all this was going on in Peking, Weidenreich, at the American Museum of Natural History in New York, was deeply involved in his detailed study of the remains of Peking man. In a large, circular tower room overlooking Central Park, he had established a laboratory where drawings, photographs, casts and comparative material drawn from the resources of the museum were spread out on worktables. He had already published several major contributions to a thorough understanding of the anatomy of various segments of the fossil array. Now he was engaged in his magnum opus, a study of the skull itself. Although he sorely missed having the original specimens to work with, he did have his detailed observations and measurements of the fossils made while he was still in China. He was able therefore to proceed with a minimum of frustration.

Although he had been forced to leave his post in Peking, he still held his professorship at the Peking Union Medical College made possible by continued financial support from the China Medical Board of the Rockefeller Foundation. It was the generosity of this institution that had for many years contributed immeasurably to Chinese education and research.

I remember vividly Weidenreich's appearance in my office when he first learned of the disastrous loss of the fossils. Ordinarily he was a very self-contained man, not given to emotional displays, but on this occasion, although outwardly controlled, he was clearly deeply shaken. Most if not all the information he had came to him from the New York office of the Rockefeller Foundation's China Medical Board, but it was clearly conflicting and inaccurate. One story related that the footlockers containing the fossils had arrived safely at Chingwangtao for transfer to the S.S. *President Harrison*. But as I have already mentioned, the S.S. *President Harrison* never reached Chingwangtao since it had sunk en route to this port.

Another story, which made somewhat more sense and which we tended to accept, was that the footlockers containing the fossils had been assigned to the last group of Marines to be evacuated before the Japanese took over all installations in Peking. En route to Tientsin, the train bearing the

Marines and their baggage was halted by Japanese troops, who ransacked the luggage, including the lost lockers. As a result, the fossils were scattered and lost.

Since communication with Peking was impossible after the war broke out, certainly for Weidenreich, there was little hope, when we heard the news, of discovering the truth or of recovering any of the apparently dispersed fossils. There was nothing to do but resign ourselves and hope that when hostilities ceased the matter could again be taken up and properly investigated.

Unfortunately, when the war with Japan came to an end, conditions in China remained chaotic. The Chinese, themselves engaged in a devastating civil war, were in no position or mood to begin any investigations of what had happened to Peking man. Weidenreich nevertheless did try again in 1947 and 1948 to stimulate action on the matter. He wrote to Washington for more precise information, but with little success. Encouraged by Fairservis' feat of discovering the Solo skull in the Japanese Emperor's Household Museum, he tried to get the authorities in Washington to send him to Peking on an investigative mission. In this, too, he failed to arouse any effective interest.

In the meantime yet another reverberation had reached us; but, like all the others, it subsided into a ripple. In November 1945, Dr. Frank Whitmore, a staff geologist with the United States Army in Tokyo, had written to Dr. Tilly Edinger at Harvard:

> November 8—We have just recovered at Tokyo University a collection of bones and artifacts from the famous *Sinanthropus pekinensis* site at Chou Kou Tien, near Peking. Also the original records of Davidson Black's research there. Also the complete original plans of the excavation and their financial records 1927–1938. We want to return all this to its owner, Peking Union Medical College, and today I'm going to scour around to see how best it can be done.

Two weeks later Whitmore wrote in more detail:

> But speaking of publicity, the *Sinanthropus* deal is
> really hot stuff. . . . I went out to Tokyo University where
> the collection was, and saw Professor H. Suzuki about it.
> He said he didn't know anything about it. I asked him
> the same question again . . . and he said, well, he *had*
> heard of it but didn't know where it was. I asked him a
> third time, and he hissed—said he'd go and look around.
> He was back in five minutes with the collection, which
> includes some chipped stones and blacked antlers, found
> with the *Sinanthropus* bones, and many more advanced
> implements and ornaments from higher levels in the
> Chou Kou Tien cave. . . .

These bones and artifacts that Whitmore found in
Tokyo had presumably not been considered precious enough
to be shipped off with the *Sinanthropus* fossils, and had been
left in the laboratory at the Peking Union Medical College.
That they had been confiscated by the Japanese even though
they were of minor interest amply confirms the fears of the
Chinese and the Americans that the Peking man fossils
would have been seized if they had been left in the laboratory. And the last-minute effort to move them to a safer
lodging now seems clearly justified.

Yet, in the light of Dr. Whitmore's success in recovering
some of the confiscated Chou Kou Tien material, the safer
course might have been to leave the major fossils in Peking.
In that case they would have been collected by the Japanese
as rare booty and transferred with every caution for their
safety and preservation to Tokyo, where Dr. Whitmore
might have reclaimed them. Another chilling thought is,
what if our atomic bomb had exploded over Tokyo instead
of Nagasaki?

One other version of the fate of the relics of Peking man
surfaced in March 1951—eighteen months after the Communist take-over of China—and involved me in a very personal and totally unexpected way. At that time, the Com-

munist press printed a story charging that the American Museum of Natural History had secretly acquired and stored the fossils. As chairman of the Department of Anthropology, I was placed in a questionable position. The item was picked up by newspapers around the world, and *The New York Times* carried an account. I immediately issued a complete denial, which *The New York Times* printed. In the following year, the same story was broadcast from China at least two more times. I didn't bother to deny the later versions since the repetitions had begun to look like convenient propaganda. And I assumed that any reasonable colleague reading such nonsense would realize the absurdity and futility of such an allegation. What could one do with such world-famous specimens if they had been illictly acquired? Any showing or scientific use of them would have been like exhibiting a stolen "Mona Lisa." And, surely, they had no aesthetic appeal that I might have gratified by a secret and solitary enjoyment of them.

I did, however, uncover a clue to the way this story might have originated. Shortly before Weidenreich died, he had been visited in his laboratory by a well-known English paleontologist, Professor D. M. S. Watson. Watson told me that on his return to London he had invited some of his graduate students to tea in his office and described some of the interesting things he had seen in the collections at the American Museum of Natural History. He also mentioned that he had called on Weidenreich, who had shown him the skull of Peking man. But, as Watson later explained to me, he had inadvertently not made it clear to the students that Weidenreich had shown him merely the *casts* of Peking man, not the original fossils. One of the young men, a German with Communist leanings, later left London and went to China. Watson concluded that this former student, not knowing that the skull was only a plaster replica, had told some Chinese paleontologists that Watson had seen Peking man in the United States, at the American Museum of Natural History.

2

DRAGON BONES

The transformation of the osseous remains of the men and women of Chou Kou Tien into virtually immortal evidence of their former existence took thousands of years. Bit by bit their organic substance had been leached out, and atom by atom mineral substitutes had slowly replaced them, thus exactly preserving the outer structure and shape of the original bones. Paleontologists call this process petrification. (It is not the only way that fossils are produced: Experts include in the broad category of fossils such relics of former organic life as imprints, natural mummification, and even soft tissue frozen for thousands of years in the permafrost layers in the Arctic.) Petrified and hard, the bones of Peking man had remained impervious to decay. The primitive men of whom they had once been a part had disappeared off the face of the earth, just as their predecessors and all but their latest followers had vanished in the course of evolution. Leaving no traces that had any obvious meaning to their modern successors, they were long forgotten and might never have existed as far as anyone knew.

The "racial memory" that Jung and others have suggested as a kind of archive where experiences from our distant past are stored can be of no help here. It was only a little over a century ago that fossils like these suddenly took on meaning and significance, opening up an expanding vista into man's past and the path to his present condition. For millennia, man had been finding fossils and crude stone tools, but their accidental discoverers could make little out of them, no more than an illiterate savage can make sense of a printed page. Although the visible artifice of a stone tool did demand some explanation—usually as the result of a thunderbolt or the work of a god or, by Lucretius, as a relic of a previous age—fossil bones were generally cast aside as the obvious remains of animals and of no interest, although there are a few instances of some having been treasured simply for their oddity.

It was not until the eighteenth century that geologists and paleontologists had begun to recognize animal fossils for what they were, and by the end of that century and in the first half of the nineteenth they had achieved considerable insight into the succession of the extinct organisms they represented. Yet the concept that man, also, might have had extinct and fossilized precursors did not at first suggest itself to these pioneers in uncovering the life of the past. What we now know to be the first human fossil to be preserved was Gibraltar man, unearthed in 1848 and followed by Neanderthal man in 1856. Although the Gibraltar fossils were published, they aroused relatively little interest since there was no accepted scientific frame of reference within which to assess their significance. This failure is reminiscent of the neglect of Mendel's fundamental discoveries in genetics until science had reached a stage where their value could be appreciated and so serve as the foundation for an amazing and rapid series of developments.

The Neanderthal discovery was similarly on its way to oblivion. Although it had aroused somewhat more interest and speculation than had the Gibraltar finds, Rudolf Virchow, one of the leading pathologists of his time and highly respected in European medical research, had declared that the fossil's peculiar form and structure did not indicate a more primitive and extinct type of man, but merely a pathological form of modern man. It was not until Darwin's publication of *The Origin of Species* in 1859 that attention was focused on the possibility that man, too, might have left a fossil record of his progress through time and evolution, just as all other forms of life had done. The Gibraltar and Neanderthal discoveries now took on meaning and were quickly cited as evidence that man had not been created as he now is, once and for all, but had gone through various progressive stages which, if they could be discovered in the fossilized remains of early man and his predecessors, would lead us back to his origin from some primate form.

Thomas Henry Huxley, the grandfather of Aldous and Julian, was an early convert to Darwin's evolutionary theory and became one of its major prophets. When he examined the Neanderthal fossil, he was deeply impressed and described it as apelike and different from any living man. Nowadays, in the light of our present knowledge and from our experience with a comparatively abundant array of manlike or hominid fossils—covering at least 4 to 5 million years and possibly 10 million or more if we accept a couple of somewhat controversial fossils—the Neanderthal specimen suggests to most specialists a far from apelike appearance. But, regardless of the assessment of the Neanderthal man, its recognition as a fossil and extinct form of man aroused great interest, not only in paleontological and anthropological circles but among laymen as well. From then on, such discoveries became increasingly informative, and more and more effort was made to unearth new ones.

Up to the end of the nineteenth century sporadic finds of fossil man were announced from time to time, but all the pre–*Homo sapiens* types belonged in the Neanderthal category. Although they confirmed the existence of this predecessor of modern man and established a concept of his range of variation, they threw little or no light on the long sequence of antecedent forms leading back to the beginnings of the hominid line.

Then, in 1891–92, Dr. Eugène Dubois, a Dutch physician in the government service of Java, made a profound penetration into the past with his discovery of fossil remains that he named *Pithecanthropus erectus*. Dubois had chosen to work in Java because of his conviction that it would prove to be a rich area for paleontological exploration. He was right. This first major published fossil discovery outside the European area consisted of a skullcap, several teeth and a femur. The skullcap, fragmentary as it was, clearly was primitive compared to *Homo sapiens*. Neanderthal man was far closer to the standards of modern man. By the same token, it was obvious that *Pithecanthropus* had evolved a considerable way from the apelike level that was then used as a kind of base from which to measure human change. His brain size, for example, was distinctly below the average of both present-day and Neanderthal populations, but about twice as large as that of even the large anthropoid apes. The skull was distinctly flat with little or no rising forehead and with a pronounced shelflike brow edged with a heavy bone structure.

These primitive and apelike features justified the name *Pithecanthropus*, taken from the Greek for "ape man"; *erectus* was added because the femur found near the skullcap was indistinguishable from that of modern man, its form and size indicating clearly that it was fully adapted for upright posture and a two-legged gait. In fact, the *Pithecanthropus* femur was so human that it seemed to some of the experts of the day to be incongruous with so apelike a skull. At a time when there were only a handful of human fossils known, and these mostly of Neanderthal man, the expectation was that the fossil record would show a correlated series of gradual and harmonious changes in all parts of the body. Thus, one anticipated a progressive adaptation to erect posture *pari passu* with a comparable increase in brain size. But here was a creature who stood and walked as we do, but with a skull remarkably primitive and apelike, a massive protruding jaw and a brain but little more than half the size of ours. This apparent incongruity led some scientists to suggest that the femur did not belong to the skull and that their juxtaposition was simply fortuitous. In the light of more recent discoveries of scores of remains of even earlier hominids, we now know that human evolution has followed a path that Earnest Hooton once called asymmetric. That is to say, posture and gait developed a manlike character while the brain lagged behind in reaching *Homo sapiens* size. One explanation is that increase in brain size reflects the response to the stimuli and pressures that the new posture brought into operation, and would therefore follow on the adaptation to upright gait. Moreover, chemical analysis of the fluorine content of the skull and femur proved that they were of the same age. It is now generally accepted that *Pithecanthropus erectus* had a fully upright posture despite his somewhat primitive brain size.

During the early twentieth century a number of additional traces of Neanderthal man turned up in various European sites, serving to enrich the details of an already known type. But it would be another thirty years before another discovery of man's past of equal age and significance was made, and a new era of fossil enrichment began.

This new chapter started with two almost contemporaneous finds, one in South Africa, the other in China, although neither of these places had previously yielded fossils of interest regarding the evolution of man. The South African discovery was the now-famous *Australopithecus africanus*. It was in 1925 that Professor Raymond Dart announced his reappearance, after more than a million years underground, near Taungs. Although he was immature, with most of his milk teeth still intact, it is now clear from numerous related specimens that Dart had in his hands a representative of the earliest hominid, or manlike creature, then known. But whatever Dart may have thought privately, he was not then prepared to announce this role for the newcomer on the stage. Although he cautiously pointed out some of its curiously hominid traits, the very name he gave it meant, in Greek, the southern monkey or ape from Africa, and it was only later that he was prepared to defend its right to be placed near the roots of the human line of evolution. Certainly, the distinguished experts of the day, such as Sir Arthur Keith, gave him no encouragement to do so. And even in 1931, when Earnest Hooton, one of the leading physical anthropologists in the United States, published his masterly book *Up From the Ape*, he left out *Australopithecus* as a possible precursor of the human line. Now this find and all the other *Australopithecines* discovered since Dart's first announcement are universally accepted by the experts as representing an early stage in the hominid lines.

When, almost at the same time, Davidson Black in Peking identified a molar tooth as belonging to a new type of primitive man, his publication received a far different reception. Black named the newly discovered fossil from Chou Kou Tien *Sinanthropus pekinensis*—the Chinese man from Peking—and this ancient "Chinese" captured the attention of the world, not only anthropologists and other scientists dedicated to the study of human evolution, but the general public as well. *The New York Times* covered this and the subsequent discoveries, for it was just after the Scopes trial, and evolution was a hot subject.

It very soon became evident that Peking man was a distinct and significant form of early man; that the population he represented had a place in the sequence leading to modern man. The only type that was generally recognized as even earlier and definitely more primitive was *Pithecanthropus*, from Java. The South African discovery of the preceding year had not yet challenged this assessment.

The story of how Peking man came to be found at all is interesting in itself. For some years it had been well known among paleontologists in China that the "drugstore" in a Chinese town was a likely place to find petrified fossils. For it was here the peasants brought for sale the "dragon" bones they found in their fields. What the peasants did not know, but the paleontologists did, was that these so-called dragon bones were fossils of extinct animals. For centuries they had had a recognized place in the traditional pharmacopeia of China, and they were in great demand for their medicinal properties. In China, unlike the West, the dragon was considered a benevolent beast and a deity who ruled over rivers, the seas and the rain. Temples where his worship was celebrated were widespread, and his aid was sought during periods of drought. Early in Chinese tradition he had become the symbol of the perfect man, the Son of Heaven, and the Emperor. Dragons embellished the throne, appeared on the imperial banner and were carved in stone to decorate public places. A couple of legendary emperors were even said to have been conceived by the embraces of Dragons.[1]

Dragons' teeth and dragons' bones were consequently greatly valued. Back in the fifth century A.D., there were already well-established recipes for their use. Lei Hiao (420–477 A.D.), for example, recommended dragon bones of five colors as best, and those of a black color as least desirable. Those collected by women he described as useless. The bones were prepared as follows:

> First boil some aromatic herbs. Wash the bone twice in hot water, then reduce it to powder and place it in bags of thin stuff. Take two young swallows and, after removing their entrails, stuff the bags into the swallows and hang them over a spring. After one night take the bags out of the swallows, remove the powder and mix it with a preparation for strengthening the kidneys. The effect of such a medicine is as if it were divine.

By the 1920's the recipe had been simplified. An apothecary told J. G. Andersson, a well-known Swedish geologist, that all you had to do was pulverize the bones or teeth and add the powder to a cup of tea. It had so wide a

[1] *Children of the Yellow Earth*, J. Gunnar Andersson, 1934. For this information on dragon bones and other circumstances in the discovery of Peking man, I am indebted to Dr. Andersson.

use for such a variety of ailments, it could scarcely be called a specific. It was prescribed for dysentery, gallstones, fevers, paralysis, women's maladies, malaria, liver diseases and a number of other complaints. It was even supposed to appease unrest of the heart and disquiet of the soul. Given the demand for such a divine panacea, one wonders that any fossils were left for the paleontologist to unearth. Certainly, this recycling must have destroyed a vast quantity of valuable material.

One of the first to use this bizarre source of fossil data was Dr. K. A. Haberer, a German naturalist collecting in China. His purchases of dragon bones from apothecaries in a number of cities, including Peking, were published by Professor Max Schlosser in 1903. One of the specimens was a tooth that Schlosser was uncertain whether to identify as an ape's or a man's. Nothing much was made of this discovery, and not until twenty-three years later was it recognized as a clue that had been missed. As this illustrates, fossils collected second- or third-hand in drugstores have only a limited value since they lack the documentation needed for their orientation in time and association with other forms of life.

It was, however, this common knowledge among the foreign geologists and paleontologists who were active in China in the early twentieth century that led geologist J. Gunnar Andersson to explore the drugstores as a source of information about the fossils of China. He had, in 1914, been appointed by the Chinese government to survey the coal and ore resources of the country and to act in an advisory capacity on mining and geological problems. He was obviously a man of great energy, strong convictions and wide-ranging interests. And equally important, he was able to establish warm and cooperative relations not only with fellow scientists working in China but with the Chinese officials who were supporting his work.

Andersson's interest in the Chinese past was expanding rapidly. He has recorded that he began making active use of the drugstores for clues to fossil sites as early as 1917. In that year he persuaded the Geological Survey of China to identify promising areas for paleontological exploration by following the pathways of the dragon-bone traffic back to their origins. Circulars were distributed to mission stations and to various individuals who might be aware of such local activities. The strategy was successful in opening up a number of rich sites to Andersson and his colleagues. And, from their labors, a considerable literature embodying a vast new knowledge of the organic past in China was assembled.

Andersson, of course, was thoroughly aware of the fossils coming into the Peking apothecaries and may well have known that many of them were being excavated by the peasants at Chou Kou Tien, a town some thirty-odd miles southwest of Peking. He was, at any rate, familiar with the area because of his geological explorations there. But in 1918 he was attracted to Chou Kou Tien by a report from J. McGregor Gibb, Professor of Chemistry at Peking University, who had found some fossils there. These had come from a place known as "Chicken Bone Hill" and were apparently typical hollow bird bones. On March 22 and 23, 1918, Andersson paid another visit to Chou Kou Tien to investigate Gibb's find. Chicken Bone Hill, Chi Ku Shan in Chinese, turned out to be a red clay pillar rising out of the base of an old limestone quarry. Andersson concluded that this pillar represented an old fill in a crevice of the basic limestone. As the natives had mined the limestone for conversion into lime by burning, they had left the useless consolidated clay fill because of a local superstition that it housed evil spirits. The pillar turned out to contain, embedded within it, a multitude of bird fossils of apparently minor interest.

Andersson's belief in Chou Kou Tien as a rich source of fossils was revived in 1921. Paleontology had become increasingly fascinating to him and, feeling the need of a well-trained and able field assistant, he had persuaded the young Austrian paleontologist Otto Zdansky to transfer his researches to China that summer. Although Zdansky eventually traveled widely over China, explored a large number of sites and published a series of important discoveries, he began his paleontological excavations in China at Chou Kou Tien.

At about the same time, Dr. Walter Granger, a distinguished paleontologist at The American Museum of Natural History in New York City, had come to Peking in preparation for Roy Chapman Andrews' famous Central Asiatic Expeditions in Mongolia in the 1920's. Because of previous arrangements with the Chinese government, Granger was not permitted to carry on any scientific work in China itself. This, however, did not preclude his giving advice and assistance to the Chinese investigations under the charge of Andersson. In fact, Granger was consulted then and later by both Zdansky and Andersson on a number of faunal identifications and field techniques.

On this occasion, Andersson was anxious to make Granger's advice and expertise in excavation available to Zdansky at Chou Kou Tien, and he therefore arranged for Granger to accompany him there.

Granger was well aware of Chou Kou Tien as a dragonbone treasury, for it was from him that I first learned, years later, about paleontologists haunting the drugstores of Peking looking for fossil rarities. On their arrival, Andersson and Granger joined Zdansky and were pursuing their examination of the Chicken Bone Hill site when they were accosted by a local resident who said, "There's no use staying here any longer. Not far from here there is a place where you can collect much larger and better dragons' bones."

Always receptive to dragon-bone clues, Andersson questioned his Chinese informant with care and was so impressed by his apparent reliability that he immediately decided to take his advice. The three men then gathered up their equipment and followed their informant to the recommended site in a nearby abandoned quarry. Along one vertical side of the surrounding wall, facing north, they could easily see a deep horizontal fissure about thirty feet above the floor of the quarry. It was about five or six feet thick at its exposed face and was filled with fragments of limestone, clay and the bones of large animals, all more or less solidified. To one side of the horizontal crevice there was another, perpendicular one, extending downward like a root. This was the place their Chinese informant recommended for finding dragon bones. Its Chinese name was Lao Niu Kou.

Andersson relates that in a very short time they collected the jaws of a pig and a stag, and the next day, a richer array including rhinoceros teeth and the jawbones of hyenas and bears. They now knew they had struck pay dirt and had excellent chances of assembling a rich collection of extinct animals that could throw light on the evolution of the Chinese mammalian fauna. That night they drank toasts to their future success.

After another day or two, which permitted Granger to instruct Zdansky in the new techniques of excavation that he had developed, Zdansky remained on his own at Chou Kou Tien for several weeks exploring the crevices of Lao Niu Kou. He completed this first season of exploration in the late summer of 1921, having found only animal, mainly mammalian, fossils. The results were promptly published in the *Bulletin* of the Geological Survey of China.

Two years later Zdansky was back again at Chou Kou Tien at the request of Andersson, who has described his deep-seated conviction that something more than mammalian fossils was tucked away somewhere in the fills of the ancient caves and crevices of the limestone hill. The haul this time was rich, consisting of at least twenty different species that were at the time dated as far back as the beginning of the Pleistocene period, well over a million years ago. There were large felines as well as rhinoceroses, horses, bears, hyenas, saber-toothed tigers, buffalo, dingoes, beavers, hares and even wolves. Most of the species found were long extinct although a few, such as the deer, bear and dog, were not too different from modern varieties.

But perhaps the most important discovery of that season's work did not become known until three years later, in 1926. The fossils excavated in these field expeditions had been sent to Upsala, Sweden, where a laboratory had been set up to process and study them. In 1926 Andersson wrote to Professor C. Wiman, who was in charge of the laboratory, asking him to send any important new results that might have emerged from the studies then in progress. Andersson wanted to have some significant announcement to make at a scientific meeting he had arranged to be held in Peking on October 22 of that year, in honor of the visit of the Crown Prince and Princess of Sweden, who were on a round-the-world trip and were due in China at that time.

Wiman, of course, responded with new details of *Helopus*, a dinosaur that Andersson and his assistants had uncovered in Shantung, and with reports on an unusual kind of fossil giraffe and a snouted horse. But, along with this interesting information, Andersson also received a communication from Zdansky that proved to be the stunning announcement he wanted to make.

Zdansky wrote that he had two teeth—a molar and a premolar (bicuspid)—from the Chou Kou Tien diggings. The molar, he had identified on the site as possibly an anthropoid ape tooth. The premolar he had discovered in the collection only after his return to Upsala in Sweden. This apparently threw new light on the identification of the teeth and, as a result, he reported that they were manlike and assigned them to *Homo sapiens*. It was a moment of great triumph for Andersson when he announced before his distinguished audience—which included some of the leading scientists working in China—that the teeth reported by Zdansky were in his opinion hominid, or manlike. He went on to say that, although the evidence was incomplete, he felt that it justified all the work, for more than a decade, that he and his colleagues had been pursuing in China. To his audience, familiar with the age of the Chou Kou Tien deposit, this was a startling announcement. Some of them reacted negatively. In particular, Andersson received a letter from Père Teilhard de Chardin expressing great caution.

Père Teilhard, who now has world fame in intellectual circles for his interpretation of evolution and its future direction, was then in China carrying on important field studies with his fellow Jesuit and scientific colleague Père Emile Licent. Since 1914 Père Licent, like Andersson, had been searching for fossils and following every clue he encountered. This scientific research and exploration was in the tradition of his Jesuit predecessors, who had from their first contacts with China been active in collecting a broad corpus of observations on Chinese life and in pursuing scientific studies. By 1922 Père Licent had become so involved that he required assistance in following the potentially important leads he had uncovered. For this reason he invited Père Teilhard to join him in his Chinese studies. Père Teilhard had been well trained in paleontology and had published a number of important papers in his field. His interests were broad enough to include fossil man and archaeology. In fact, he had taken considerable interest in the Piltdown man discovery in England, and had written on that subject as well.

His study of evolution, which was basic to all his scientific work, had, however, created problems for him in the Church. When I first met Père Teilhard about forty years ago, he made no mention of any such difficulties, but later, after I had come to know him better, he revealed some of the tensions he had suffered. One of the disciplinary restrictions he suffered was being forbidden to conduct mass. I remember on one occasion his scarcely concealed jubilation as he described to me the special audience he had been granted with Pope John. He had been called to discuss the possibility of a reversal of the Church's traditional hostility toward evolution. After a warm and sympathetic reception, he had left with a strong feeling that at last his dedication to the study of evolution would no longer be frowned upon by the Church, and that his own tribulations would end. In his optimism, he declared that he expected a papal bull to be issued in the near future that would, in effect, accept the validity of evolution. The bull, when it finally appeared, did not go to the lengths that Père Teilhard had earnestly hoped for, but it did acknowledge some degree of legitimacy in the study of evolution to which he had devoted so much of his life.

Aside from his distinguished career, Père Teilhard possessed a distinguished presence. I remember on my first meeting him thinking that his lean, bony face with its beak-like nose was like the carving of a medieval knight that one might see on the sarcophagi in ancient French churches. Even his manner had an unusual charm. Toward the end of his life he spent long periods of time in New York City, where he had a number of close friends. He occupied and worked in an office on the top floor of the Wenner-Gren Foundation on East 71st Street. He is buried on the grounds of the Marist Seminary near Hyde Park on the Hudson.

Back in 1926, Père Teilhard had already completed a series of excavations in the Ordos region of western China and had discovered traces of Paleolithic man there. His authority was well established and, consequently, his letter to Andersson after the first announcement of a hominid find at Chou Kou Tien might have shaken anyone less confident. He wrote:

> I have reflected much on the photographs which you so kindly showed me and I feel that it would not be right, and still less friendly, to conceal from you what I think of them.
>
> As a matter of fact, I am not fully convinced of their supposed human character. Even the rootless assumed pre-molar, which at first sight seemed most convincing, may be one of the last molars of some carnivore, and the same is true of the other tooth, unless the roots are distinctly four in number.
>
> Even if, as I hope, it can never be proved that the Chou Kou Tien teeth belong to a beast of prey, I fear it

can never be absolutely demonstrated that they are human. It is necessary to be very cautious since their nature is undetermined.

I have not seen the specimens, however, and since I place great confidence on Zdansky's paleontological experience, I hope most intensely that my criticisms will prove unfounded. I have only wished to be very frank with you.

As I repeat these words of his, written almost fifty years ago, my memory of Père Teilhard's honesty and concern, his forthrightness softened by innate delicacy, comes back vividly. But he was not alone in that audience in having doubts about this momentous announcement. A. W. Grabau, another distinguished paleontologist associated with the National Geological Survey of China, expressed similar uncertainty.

In fact, this was perhaps the prevailing reaction around the world when, at the end of the same year, 1926, Professor Davidson Black of the Peking Union Medical College published, both in the English scientific magazine *Nature* and in the American, *Science*, the report on his study of the teeth, which Andersson had turned over to him for an expert judgment. Black's conclusion was that these were hominid. This identification did indeed bear out the claim that Zdansky had for the first time found evidence for a truly primitive man's having once existed in China. For it was abundantly clear from the geological evidence and from the associated fossil animals that whatever creature had possessed these teeth had lived a very long time ago. Black cited Andersson and Zdansky's opinion, based on the associated fauna, that this man might have existed at the end of the Pliocene, which by the then-current dating would have meant well over a million years ago. Black himself was a bit more conservative, stating, "It is possible, however, in the light of recent research that the horizon represented by this site may be lower Pleistocene age." This assignment to the geological period following the Pliocene would have reduced the estimated age to something less than a million years, but it still left the newcomer with a very considerable antiquity worthy of respect. In Black's own words:

> Whether it be of late Tertiary [Pliocene] or of early Quaternary [Pleistocene] age, the outstanding fact remains that for the first time on the Asiatic continent north of the Himalayas, archaic hominid fossil material has been recovered accompanied by complete and certain geological data. The actual presence of early man in eastern Asia is therefore now no longer a matter of conjecture.

The conjecture Black was referring to was a theory then current that the evolution of man from a primate ancestor had taken place in the region north of the Himalayas. A decade before, W. D. Mathews, a leading paleontologist at The American Museum of Natural History, had developed and published the hypothesis that the seat of man's emergence and the center of his dispersion was located in that region. Even earlier, and perhaps influential in Mathews' speculations, Henry Fairfield Osborn had published conclusions suggesting that Central Asia had been the center of dispersion for a number of distinct faunal lineages. It was, in fact, this conviction that had led Roy Chapman Andrews of The American Museum of Natural History to organize his famous Central Asiatic Expeditions to explore the Mongolian area for traces of early man. Although Andrews found a number of important fossils, including the well-known dinosaur eggs, early man eluded him.

One of the reasons this area seemed potentially rich in clues to human evolution was the discovery of extinct fossil apes in the Siwalik hills along the Himalayan border. Some of these were the *Dryopithecines* that Professor William K. Gregory, among others, had seen not only as possible ancestors to the modern ape but as relatives of still-undiscovered primates closer to the human line. Black was apparently of the same opinion as Mathews. He had written along these lines, reasoning that the elevation of the Himalayas had clearly modified the environment, which in turn might well have necessitated adaptive changes in the local primates that could have led to the emergence of a hominid line.

Although clearly Black was convinced that these fossil teeth from Chou Kou Tien belonged to some form of primitive man, of what then seemed a most impressive age, he did not in his first announcement give it either a generic or a specific name. But apparently in the circle of paleontologists and geologists working in Peking, it was known as the "Peking man."

By now, of course, it was obvious to everyone involved that a most intensive continuation of the exploration of the site at Chou Kou Tien was essential. If a couple of hominid teeth of such antiquity had already been excavated, the chances were excellent that more abundant and conclusive fossils were to be found there, for only a small fraction of the potential "pay dirt" had been explored. Andersson, who had immediately proposed a large-scale operation, was encouraged by the enthusiastic response to his suggestion, which was promptly taken up by the Geological Survey of China, working in cooperation with Black, who represented the Peking Union Medical College. The Rockefeller Foundation, through its China Medical Board, took responsibility for funding the project.

For Davidson Black this discovery and its consequences were to be the fulfillment of many years of preparation and research. He had gone out to China shortly after the First World War, in which he had served as a captain in the Canadian Army Medical Corps. The move provided him with the opportunity he had been seeking for some years, to pursue his dedicated interest in anthropology and the evolution of man. It also appealed to his deep-seated sense of adventure, for China was not only a vast, unknown and en-

ticing area to many young Americans, it was also a region
where much pioneering scientific research could be done.

Black's background of experience and training had
fitted him admirably for the course he was now pursuing.
Born in Toronto, Canada, on July 25, 1884, he had as a
youth enjoyed the adventure and excitement of exploring
the wilds of Canada. Among his early efforts were trips on
the Kawartha Lakes, where he became so expert a canoeist
that later, while still a high school student, he was able to
take a job with the Hudson Bay Company, carrying supplies
to northern Ontario. For weeks he traveled alone on dangerous rivers, making portages and shooting rapids. The only
people he encountered were the local Indians, whose language he learned and whose friend he became, even acquiring the Indian name of Mushkemush Kemit, or "Little White
Rat," in recognition of his quick and sudden movements like
the muskrat. Later he prospected for gold and on one ex-
pedition was able to save his life during a forest fire that
surrounded him only by standing in a lake for a day and two
nights. During one summer he did fieldwork for the Geological Survey of Canada and acquired, as Paul H. Stevenson, a
fellow professor, observed, "a practical knowledge of structural and stratigraphical geology that subsequently amazed
the geologists with whom he worked in connection with his
later paleontological studies, and made it possible to direct
and coordinate so satisfactorily . . . his extensive Cenozoic
researches in Asia."

Black received his medical degree at the University of
Toronto in 1906; but, because of his interest in biology, he
reversed the usual course of events by returning to the university for further study in comparative anatomy and completed his work there in 1909. With this training, he began
his career of teaching and research at the School of Medicine at Western Reserve the same year.

In the light of his future scientific preoccupation, his
visit in 1914 to the laboratory of Elliot Smith in Manchester,

England, may have been highly significant as the initial stimulus in the development of his interest in fossil man. Smith, in those days, was one of the leading authorities in neuroanatomy, and it was no doubt this fact that attracted young Black, who was already launched on a research career in this field, with several publications to his credit. Black found Smith in the middle of the fascinating problem of restoring the famous Piltdown skull. This fragmentary fossil skull had been discovered by Charles Dawson, an amateur collector, in 1911 at Piltdown, Sussex, England, and had been an object of considerable controversy from that moment. To begin with, the fossil was found in a stratum about which there was the usual disagreement. Some authorities placed the new discovery as far back as the late Pliocene. More conservative estimates settled on early Pleistocene, some 400,000 to 500,000 years ago. No hominid fossils as old as this had ever before been found in England, which alone might well have created enough excitement. But one of the initial problems was the restoration of the complete skull from the fragments that were found, consisting of the left side of the lower jaw, containing teeth, and four or five pieces of the skull vault. The jaw was very primitive— apelike in fact—but the rest of the skull was unquestionably that of a man, or a hominid. The contrast between these two skull sections was striking, but it could be rendered more or less so by the way the vault fragments were fitted together. Obviously, the more disharmonic, the greater the question that they actually belonged to the same individual. If they did, then of course the interpretation of the manner in which human evolution had occurred would be profoundly affected. For a well-developed, manlike skull vault with a large brain capacity to be associated with a very primitive jaw with apelike teeth and masticatory function would suggest an anatomical relationship of those two aspects of the skull that seemed contradictory. It was in fact this discrepancy in the Piltdown skull, as well as the presumed disharmony between the femur and the skull of *Pithecanthropus*, that influenced Professor Earnest Hooton of Harvard in developing his theory of asymmetric evolution.

The initial reconstruction by Professor Smith Woodward, a geologist, produced a skull that minimized but by no means eliminated the discrepancy. It had a cranial capacity of about 1100 c.c., which is well below the average for modern man but distinctly greater than the cubage for the most primitive man known at that time, *Pithecanthropus*. This reconstruction was immediately challenged by the leading English authority on human evolution, Sir Arthur Keith. Keith was an anatomist who had a rich experience in the study of the fossil remains of early man. Working from his more detailed knowledge of the anatomy of a skullcap, he reconstructed and restored the original form of the Piltdown skull and dramatically presented his results at a meeting of experts in the field. This new version was a far more developed type of cranial vault, differing much less than Woodward's from *Homo sapiens*, and of course emphasizing the inherent disharmony with the associated apelike jaw.

One aspect of this problem of skull reconstruction was its effect on the interpretation of the brain enclosed within it. The only way any knowledge of the evolution of the brain may be obtained is from the size of the skull vault and from the internal surface where the imprint of the contours of the brain is preserved in the bone. These unfortunately do not tell us about the significant developments taking place inside the brain. But since the brain does not fossilize and the cells are all lost, the remaining scraps of evidence are all that survive and thus take on added importance. For this reason Keith's reconstruction, which differed materially from Woodward's, sparked a vigorous, and even at times bitter, controversy between two groups of adherents. To test Keith's claims as an expert, it was suggested that he try out his reconstruction technique on a similar assemblage of fragments broken off from a skull that was well-documented but unknown to him. He consented to the test and produced a reconstructed skull that agreed admirably with the original. Naturally, the brain casts made from Woodward's and Keith's versions of the Piltdown skull differed considerably and influenced the deductions to be drawn from such evidence. Elliot Smith, as one of the leading neurologists in England, had become involved very early in the dispute and sided on the whole with Woodward. He was in the midst of it all when Black visited him in the summer of 1914. Stevenson, who knew Black intimately and was his associate in anatomy at the Peking Union Medical College, was convinced that this firsthand introduction to the problems associated with the unraveling of human evolution had played a major role in determining Black's future career and scientific interests. In Stevenson's words,

> . . . under the spell of the tremendous fascination of this problem was born the greatest of the several personages of Davidson Black—namely, Davidson Black the Anthropologist. Here was the call from the unknown for which his restless spirit had been waiting. A call that came at once as a challenge and an opportunity; one of those rare opportunities that come only to those prepared. . . . All of his previous interests and experiences immediately and naturally fell into their self-appointed places in this broad foundation of correlated qualifications that guided his approach to the new problem now uppermost in his mind.

Despite Stevenson's exuberance, there is a solid justice in his appraisal of the effect produced by Black's immersion in the excitement of one of the most bitterly fought controversies in the history of human paleontology. Fortunately, Black was unaware of the major flaw in the whole issue. The Piltdown fossil was a fake—the only one, to my knowledge, that has ever been perpetrated. This was discovered many years later, in 1955, when K. P. Oakley and J. S. Weiner, two distinguished British anthropologists, published their findings on a reexamination of the specimen. By that time, testing for the amount of fluorine absorbed by bones and fossils buried in the ground had become an established method of determining relative age. Thus, if two separate fossils lying in the same stratum have equivalent values for fluorine content, it can be assumed they are contemporaneous. If, however, the fluorine contents are significantly different, it can only mean that they are not coeval in that stratum. When the elephant and hippopotamus teeth found in association with the Piltdown man remains were tested, it was found that the former contained far more fluorine—which, of course, contradicted the assumption that the Piltdown fossil was as ancient as they were. In fact, the tests indicated that the Piltdown fragments were modern. This led to further studies of the jaw, which was clearly shown to be a chimpanzee's, dyed with chemicals and otherwise treated to give an impression of great age.

The publication of Oakley and Weiner's *Piltdown Man* caused a sensation, but it did belatedly justify some of us who had for a long time regarded the specimen as improbable, not to say incredible. It brought back to prominence a paper written by G. Miller of the Smithsonian Institution back in 1915, in which he had suggested that the jaw was that of an ape. And it confirmed Weidenreich's strong conviction that the "early man" was a "chimæra" and should not be taken seriously. Thus Piltdown man, or *Eoanthropus dawsoni*, disintegrated.

It is not, under the circumstances, an unreasonable question to ask how such distinguished and knowledgeable experts as Keith, Woodward and Smith—men of undisputed authority—could have been taken in by what now appears to have been an obvious fraud. And why were so many, if not all, equivalent authorities in other countries so readily persuaded? But these are not easy questions to answer. Clearly, the discrepancy between the jaw and skull was apparent from the beginning. Perhaps scientists sometimes lose sight of objective goals when they are subtly influenced by personal identification with the objects of their interest and moved by a sense of nationalism and local pride. Keith was quite frankly exultant at the discovery in England of a fossil that outdated anything that had been found in France or elsewhere in Europe, and this feeling was shared by other English scientists of the time. A similar chauvinism found expression in the efforts of the Argentinian Ameghino to claim hominid identity for fossils he uncovered in his country. Nor is a trace of it altogether absent in France, where a rich array of the relics of early man have been uncovered.

The issues can become intense when the discoverer or sponsor of a fossil is involved, and it has led to much unnecessary confusion. Again and again, a new discovery is hailed as unique and given its own special name to save it from being lost in a general category and assigned to an undistinguished anonymity. There is a difference between a Eugène Dubois, the discoverer of *Pithecanthropus*, or a Raymond Dart, announcing the new *Australopithecus*, and the host of forgotten names of those who found the dozens and dozens of Neanderthal remains.

But it still puzzles me that Woodward and Keith did not recognize that the bones of Piltdown man were not petrified and true fossils. Both of them had had enough experience with genuine fossils to distinguish them from relatively recent unpetrified bone.

Fame carries enormous prestige. It would have taken a courageous anthropologist even outside England to question the authority of Sir Arthur Keith. Some did, but many did not.

But back in 1914, when Black had fallen under the spell of the Piltdown controversy, he was unaware that the "fossil" was flawed evidence as far as human evolution was concerned. The turning of his interests became clear after the First World War, when he was free again to resume scientific work. In his publications after settling in China, one can trace an increasing commitment to anthropological research and to the problems of human evolution. It was this devotion that made him a natural choice for Andersson when he needed expert advice on the identification of hominid fossils. There was no one in Peking better qualified, and certainly no one more eager to participate in the study of such remains.

Thus, after the first announcement of a hominid find at Chou Kou Tien in 1926 and the establishment of a definite program to continue the exploration there, Black took responsibility for the scientific study of any hominid fossils that might turn up. Dr. V. K. Ting, a notable Chinese scientist who had created the Geological Survey of China and established the prestigious scientific series Palæontologia Sinica, where much of the scientific production in geology and paleontology was published, was named honorary director. The actual fieldwork was assigned to C. Li, a Chinese geologist, and a young Swedish paleontologist, Dr. Birger Bohlin, was imported to serve as general director of the enterprise.

That season lasted from April to October 1927, and the work progressed steadily even though the area was the scene of skirmishes between Chang Tso-lin and Yen Hsi-shan, who were waging a civil war. Banditry was rife, but it scarcely affected Li and Bohlin. The cavity where they worked contained a deposit 35 to 55 feet thick, and extended east and west for about 150 feet with a width of more than 48 feet. Altogether some 90,000 cubic feet were excavated and examined, but only a limited portion of the deposit yielded any fossils. Then, just three days before the end of the season, Bohlin found another hominid tooth—a lower molar, unworn and perfectly preserved. Its incompletely developed roots were comparable to those of the molars of eight-year-old children today.

Despite the dangers of traversing the war-torn countryside, Bohlin braved these hazards and appeared before Black, who described the encounter as follows:

On October 19th [three days after the discovery], at half-past six in the evening Bohlin came to my institution in field dress, covered with dust but beaming with pleasure. He had finished the season's work despite the war, and on October 16th he had discovered the tooth. He was himself on the spot where it was taken out of the deposits. Certainly, I was overjoyed! Bohlin came to me before he told his wife he was in Peking. He is indeed a man after my own heart and I hope you will tell Wiman how much I value his assistance for procuring Bohlin for our work in China.

And then, reflecting his own eagerness, Black is quick to find confirmation for his hopes by reporting, "Bohlin is quite certain that he will find more of *Homo pekinensis* when he begins to sift in the laboratory the material he takes home."

When Black made his formal scientific announcement of the new discovery at the end of 1927, he took a decisive step by identifying the Chou Kou Tien fossil teeth as belonging to a new and distinct genus of man—*Sinanthropus pekinensis*. This was a bold conclusion, and the reaction— where these events in Peking were being followed with interest—was mixed. Many well-qualified experts thought Black was rash to set up a new and distinct genus on the basis of a few teeth. Had he assigned the new finds to another species within the genus *Homo*, it might have been more acceptable. But a different genus implies a far greater degree of differentiation, and much more substantial evidence than it seemed to some that Black could muster. In his defense, it must be made clear that Black had examined these teeth with great care and had observed every detail of their structure.

Perhaps no part of the skeleton has been so thoroughly and meticulously analyzed by paleontologists as the teeth. The forms of cusps, roots, crests and crevices have all been studied carefully and their variations arranged in systematic patterns. This is in part because teeth are by all odds the most abundant of all fossil remains, and therefore often provide the only evidence of various extinct species, and also in part because there are quite distinctive observable patterns of tooth structure that yield very useful clues to their owner's affinity.

The following season, 1928, Bohlin returned to his exciting mission at Chou Kou Tien assisted by two very able Chinese scientists, W. C. Pei and C. C. Young. This time they came up with a much more abundant array of teeth in varying stages of development, and with fragments of the lower jaw and small parts of the skull vault that were of considerable importance. Any doubt that *Sinanthropus pekinensis* was distinctive and different from modern man was completely dispelled by these discoveries. Perhaps at first glance the most striking characteristic of these new fossil remains of the mandibles was their chinless form, which gave them a very primitive, almost apelike appearance. Black observed that the bony jaw was even more primitive than the teeth it supported.

Almost as if deliberately staged to build up to a climax, the next season—1929—finally ushered in the long–awaited and sought for skull itself. Again at the very end of the season, just before closing the diggings for the winter, W. C. Pei found in one of the caves he had opened up the "almost complete skull" of *Sinanthropus* partly imbedded in loose sand and partly solidified in a hard matrix. A telegram went off immediately to Black, who must have waited impatiently for this precious new piece of evidence to be delivered into his hands. In his preliminary report, Black stressed the wide difference between *Sinanthropus* and *Pithecanthropus*, a distinction that later investigators have minimized. Moreover, he concluded that the former was the more generalized and progressive form, suggesting that it was a more likely candidate as ancestor to modern man.

From then on, until the work at Chou Kou Tien was halted in 1937 as the result of internal political turmoil, new discoveries continued to be made. It was estimated that by 1937 at least forty different individuals were represented in the collection of teeth, skulls and long bones. This, of course, is only an estimate since it is not always easy to determine what fragments or teeth belonged together. But at that time it was the largest collection ever made of a single fossil population of hominids, and it presented a monumental task of study and analysis that would take years to complete.

Many scientists—geologists, paleontologists and anthropologists—had particpated in the long and arduous excavations at Chou Kou Tien: Andersson, Zdansky, Pei, Bohlin and Li, to mention only a few. And a number of widely known authorities, such as Père Teilhard de Chardin, the Abbé Breuil and C. C. Young, published detailed studies of the remains that were discovered. But one name alone stood out in that entire galaxy as completely identified with Peking man. This was Davidson Black. For almost a decade before his death early in 1934, he had devoted himself with complete dedication to the task he had gone to China in the hope of finding. He had ranged widely in his early apprentice years, looking for promising sites, only to end up with Peking man waiting practically at his doorstep.

When I met him in his laboratory in Peking in 1931, he was in the midst of cleaning and preparing fossil fragments. He demonstrated to me how he used a dental drill to remove the hard encrustations that clung to their surfaces. As he worked, a great cloud of fine dust ground out by the drill surrounded his head, and I asked him if he wore a mask to keep from breathing in the powder. His answer was no, and when he died there was a rumor that his lungs had been affected by the fossil dust; but the official report merely mentioned a heart condition, of which his friends said he was aware. It was for this reason, some of his closest associates said, that he had worked at night, in order to accomplish as much as possible without the distractions and strains of a daytime regime.

All of them spoke of his warmth and humanity, but I find it highly significant that some of his Chinese colleagues, in their memorial tributes, emphasized a special aspect of his character that influenced his behavior toward and relations with his Chinese coworkers. Of the four Chinese scientists who offered their eulogies, three make this same point, but none as fully as Dr. V. K. Ting.

> The last point which I should like to touch is a delicate one, but I am going to touch it nevertheless. It is frankly admitted that sometimes we find cooperation between Chinese and foreigners in scientific work rather difficult. The reasons I think are not difficult to seek. Firstly, many foreigners are suffering from a superiority complex. Subconsciously they think somewhat like this: here is a Chinese, he knows something about science, but he is a Chinese nevertheless—he is different from a European, therefore we cannot treat him in the same way. At best his manners become patronizing. On the other hand, their Chinese colleagues are suffering from an inferiority complex. They become self-conscious and supersensitive, always imagining that the foreigner is laughing at them or despising them. Ninety per cent of the troubles between Chinese and foreign colleagues working together comes from these two factors. In my dealings with Davidson Black, and I think Black's colleagues will bear me out, I never found him suffering from such a complex, and his Chinese colleagues became also free from theirs. In politics, Black was a conservative, but in his dealings with his Chinese colleagues, he forgot altogether about their nationality or race, because he realized that science was above such artificial and accidental things.

3

WHAT HE LOOKED LIKE

Virtually all people in all cultures conceive of their human ancestors as having looked much as they themselves do. It is surprising that this belief is so common because the myths of origin vary enormously, deriving man from a wide range of elements, animals and gods. Yet even where earlier versions of man are supposed to have existed, as in some American Indian myths, the final form that succeeded them all has remained unchanged. Our own Adam and Eve, created in God's image in 4004 B.C., according to Bishop Ussher's chronology, would, except for their nakedness, pass unnoticed in the present-day population. When their creation was recorded in Genesis, it would have been not much more than 3000 years since the event. This short view of man's existence is also characteristic of origin myths. Few Polynesian accounts, for example, place the appearance of man at more than about thirty generations ago, a mere 900 years at most. And in the legends of some of the native tribes of the Philippines, the creation of man is located in a somewhat misty, vague era only as far back as six or eight generations. It may be partly this abbreviated vision of man and his world that tends to suggest that, on his first emergence, he arrived in full bloom. The radical changes that converted our primate ancestor into a hominid, and which we now take for granted, are not likely to suggest themselves to people with a brief history. There would scarcely be time enough.

One of the less appreciated but nonetheless profound reorientations that modern science has brought about in our thinking about ourselves and our place in the world is in our concept of time. Archaeology has lengthened our vistas into man's cultural past, and this temporal expansion has been duplicated by enormous extensions of the earth's history by geology and astronomy and the astonishing sequences of organic adaptation discovered by paleontology. Today it is generally accepted that all forms of life, including man, have histories of change stretching over millions of years. We have become accustomed in our thinking to accept that our ancestors went through an evolutionary transformation marked at each stage by significant and visible changes. The horror and revulsion that our Victorian predecessors felt when it was suggested that such an evolutionary sequence might link us even remotely with the apes was reflected in Carlyle's rejection of Huxley's "monkey damnification" of mankind. And it was the same incredulity and horror that led Samuel Wilberforce, the Bishop of Oxford, to ask Huxley, with what he thought was devastating scorn, which of his grandparents was an ape. Huxley's answer was that he would prefer having an ape for a grandfather than the bishop.

When Peking man was recognized back in 1926 as a representative of one of the earliest forms of primitive man then known, the public, if not unanimous in its acceptance of him as an ancestral figure, was nevertheless widely interested in his discovery and curious about his appearance. The initial discoveries consisted of teeth which, important as they may be in establishing evolutionary relationships, are of little or no value in reconstructing the general appearance of the individuals to whom they belonged. The first skullcap and jaw fragments, found in 1928 and 1929, gave the experts the first inklings of the general character of the head and parts of the face. Later, as more abundant and more complete cranial specimens were excavated and fragments of the skeletons were recovered, the picture became richer and more detailed. It is now possible to present a fair approximation of what Peking man looked like in life. Certain details are missing, of course, since many segments of the skeleton were not represented in the collection of fossils.

One of the first things that might strike a modern observer is the small size of these primitive men. Stature can with considerable accuracy be calculated from the length of the leg and arm bones since these are highly correlated with it. Where all the limb bones are available, the estimates are, of course, much more exact. In fact, I have found this relationship extremely useful in forensic medicine, and not infrequently it has been a determining factor in identifying skeletons discovered under suspicious circumstances by the police. Immediately after World War II, it was one of a number of procedures I was able to employ in the identification program I established in the Graves Registration Section under the Quartermaster General. Congress had passed a law to bring back to the U.S. all men who had been killed in action or had died overseas. Unfortunately, many of the bodies—thousands in fact—had been recovered without their identification tags and had been temporarily buried in Europe and in the Pacific area. It became a major problem for the Quartermaster General to find a way of identifying them accurately in order that they might be returned to their families as the law required. One of the major characteristics that we were able to use was stature, which could be readily calculated from the limb bones.

Applying this technique to Peking man, however, was somewhat complicated by the fact that not one of the seven femora was complete. Moreover, of those that could be identified by sex, one was female and four were male. There were only two humeri, or upper arm bones, both fragmentary. Nevertheless, by a meticulous reconstruction process based on very detailed studies and comparisons, Weidenreich was able to restore with great reliability the missing parts of two male and one female femora. One of the humeri was also complete enough to permit a similar reconstruction. From these bones, the stature of the males was estimated to have been 5 feet 1½ inches, and of the female, 4 feet 8½ inches. While these figures, based as they are on an inadequate sample of arm and leg bones, are clearly only tentative, as a group average they carry considerable conviction since the remaining fragments, not used in this calculation, agree very closely with those that were. Moreover, if we take the male figure as fairly reliable, being based on and confirmed by the greater number of bones, we could normally expect to find a sex difference of the order that the figures suggest.

By our standards, then, the Peking men and women were distinctly short—at the very lowest margin of present-day variation. If we leave out as deviant groups the Pygmies and Bushmen, who average from 4 feet 7 inches to 4 feet 9 inches, the range of modern population means runs from about 5 feet to just under 6 feet, with 5 feet 6 inches representing the mode for all groups of modern *Homo sapiens*.

Compared, however, with still earlier forms of hominids, the *Australopithecines* of Africa, who can be dated at 1 to 4 million years ago, the Peking population shows a very considerable increase in size. These earlier hominids averaged around 4 feet 6 inches and are estimated to have weighed only about 60 or 70 pounds.

Although fossilized skeletal bones are relatively rare and usually fragmentary, enough evidence has been accumulated to make it possible to generalize about the transformation in body size that has characterized human evolution. There has been, in other words, a steady progressive increase from the earliest accepted hominids—the *Australopithecines*—to recent man, with Peking man standing about halfway between these two extremes. If we include the *Ramapithecus* fossils as even earlier evidence of emergent man—some 10 to 12 million years ago—the course of this progression is still further emphasized. At that stage our ancestors were even smaller, judging from the size of the jaws and teeth they have left behind. Although these anatomical developments are not as closely correlated with stature as the limb bones, they can give a general approximation that is fairly reliable.

This trend raises several questions of considerable interest. First, we should like to know the significance of this evolutionary increase in size. When we examine various other vertebrate and invertebrate lineages, it is not uncommon to find a steady progressive accretion in bulk. Take the dinosaurs, which from small beginnings ended in massive gigantic forms that astonish the visitors of the museums where their remains are reassembled. *Brontosaurus* attained a length of 65 feet, with a weight estimated to have been 30 tons. And *Brachiosaurus* towered 34 feet in height. The whale is another example of overwhelming amplification, reaching in some species the impressive length of 90 feet. But there are many more less-extreme but equally illustrative examples of this common phenomenon, sometimes called Cope's Rule after Professor E. D. Cope, a nineteenth-century pioneer paleontologist. Horses, camels, elephants and giraffes show a similar tendency, all having begun as small creatures and reaching, in our day, respectable magnitudes. And yet there are a large number of forms that have maintained their size with little change over comparable periods of time. The rodents, for example, although some species and genera show a modest tendency in this direction, have never attained any noteworthy increase in bulk size and in many cases have remained small.

Among the Primates, the order to which man and the closely related hominids belong, this progressive enlargement of body size in the course of evolution crops up repeatedly, though never in the extreme form we see in the elephants or whales. The first primates back in the Paleocene, some 60-odd million years ago, were only about the size of a small mouse. Some of them developed into larger, if not gigantic, forms. In more recent times, the family of

Pongidae, apes closely related to the hominids, have also displayed a more pronounced tendency toward increasing size. The gorilla, which is the largest of the apes, has reached the impressive weight of 400 to 500 pounds and in some cases stands close to six feet in height.

A number of suggestions have been put forward by paleontologists to account for this phenomenon. It has been assumed by some that an increase in size can be explained in terms of greater physiological efficiency. As the body increases in bulk, the surface area expands to a much lesser degree and thus, at least in warm-blooded animals, there is relatively less loss of body heat. All this means that small forms need proportionally more food and energy to maintain normal body temperature than do larger, bulkier ones.

Physical enlargement in grazing animals most certainly enables them to forage more widely; and for predators some increase in bulk can make them more effective in their attack. The probabilities, however, suggest that the complex of factors that produce this trend may well be different in distinct lineages.

It has been pointed out, however, that this tendency can lead to certain disadvantages if carried too far and may contribute to extinction and the end of the line. The fact that some small forms have also become extinct may not be used in counter-argument since there can be, and are, a variety of reasons for maladaptation and the death of a species.

All this raises the question, is man headed for an appreciable further increase in size in the course of his future evolution? The fact that there has been a progressive trend in that direction in the past does not, of course, mean that it will necessarily continue. We know too little about the nature of the phenomenon to be able to predict its course with any degree of confidence. But it brings to mind a recent phenomenon in human history that at first glance seems pertinent and that certainly has engaged the attenion and interest of many people.

This is the steady increase in stature, generation by generation, that first became noticeable in the Western world and quite recently in Japan as well. It has not infrequently been observed that suits of armor used by the warriors of the Middle Ages are generally much too small for even the average European or American to wear. And in many families it is a common observation that the sons tower above their fathers, and the daughters can't fit into any of their mothers' dresses even if they wanted to. But there is far more specific data to bear out this common observation. Measurements of army recruits in Sweden show a progressive increase in stature over the past century. Similar statistics assembled in France for an even longer period of time display the same tendency. English figures are quite explicit on the phenomenon and suggest that the process was well under way by the eighteenth century. Karl Pearson, a distinguished English biological statistician, reconstructed the statures, for example, of a relatively large series of skeletons excavated at Moorfields and Whitechapel in London and dating to the seventeenth century. The average was 5 feet 5 inches. Sir Francis Galton found that the English male two centuries later had reached a mean of 5 feet 8 inches. More recent figures show a further increase. In the United States, one of the earliest estimates goes back to the Revolutionary period, and the sampling, although it is far from complete and its age structure is unknown, provides an average of 5 feet 6 inches for soldiers and 5 feet 5 inches for sailors. Some years ago I published a paper on a study I had made of some skeletons that had been interred in the Nagel cemetery in upper New York City. This burial ground, dating back to the eighteenth century, had been neglected and then forgotten. When excavations for a new car barn were under way, the old graves were discovered again. Fortunately I managed to study some of the bones before they were reinterred. The population, judging by the names in the records, was principally English with a few Dutch. Their average height proved to be 5 feet 6 inches, about the same as the figure for the contemporary Revolutionary soldiers and a shade larger than that for the seventeenth-century Londoners. Some ninety years later, roughly three generations, the soldiers in the Union Army had reached an average of 5 feet 8½ inches. These were native-born Americans mainly of British antecedents. By the First World War, American soldiers, now including nineteenth-century immigrant strains, averaged just under 5 feet 8 inches. If we allow for the inclusion in this figure of originally shorter stocks than the English, it suggests a continuation of this progressive heightening.

A more specific bit of evidence is the data reported by Gordon Bowles on the size of Harvard freshmen, decade by decade for sixty years, beginning with the period from 1856 to 1865. The averages in sequence are as follows:

1856–1865	5 feet 8 inches
1866–1875	5 feet 8⅔ inches
1876–1885	5 feet 9 inches
1886–1895	5 feet 9½ inches
1896–1905	5 feet 9⅘ inches
1906–1915	5 feet 10 inches

When sons were compared with fathers, Bowles found a generational jump of 1.38 inches. A similar phenomenon was found in college girls, although the data does not cover as long a span of time.

One of the generally accepted explanations for this steady addition in height, generation by generation, is diet. The evidence for this is largely inferred from the fact that children on a deprived or substandard diet do not reach the height levels of better-nourished representatives of the same population, but it has never been properly assessed as a conclusive and total explanation of this trend. For one thing, there is little or no indication that the diet between 1750 and 1800 or between 1800 and 1850 had appreciably improved in England or in other Western countries where the phenomenon was taking place. Nor can one claim that the diet in Japan took a sudden and notable leap to significantly higher levels of nutritive value beginning around the 1920's;

yet it is from approximately this date that the measurements of Japanese samples show a steady increase. Today any visitor walking in Tokyo is immediately struck by the way the young Japanese loom up over their elders. Until the 1920's there had been no generational change of any significance.

As in many biological processes, normal variations in growth rate and mature size may well represent the sum total of several factors working together in a somewhat synergistic fashion. That one of these might be hybrid vigor, or heterosis, occurred to me many years ago when I made a genetic study of the descendants of the English mutineers of the H.M.S. *Bounty* and their Tahitian wives. Hybrid vigor, the genetic result of crossing independent strains of plants and animals, had been a major field of research explored by Professor E. M. East, who in 1919 wrote one of the principal formulations of the phenomenon. He had observed that when inbred strains of corn were crossed they produced an F_1 generation with a notable increase in size and productivity. This led to the use of hybridization by animal and plant breeders with much success; the family of Henry Wallace, for example, made a fortune in exploiting hybrid corn. More recently, hybrid wheat and rice have been introduced to India with a remarkable improvement in production.

In my first study of the descendants of the mutineers of the Bounty back in 1923, I worked with the colony that had migrated from Pitcairn to Norfolk Island, and was able to assemble perhaps the first demonstration of hybrid vigor in human miscegenation. The males of the first generation born on Pitcairn averaged 177.8 cm., the shortest man being 5 feet 9 inches and the tallest, 6 feet ¼ inch. The average was roughly 6.5 cm. greater than for the Tahitian males and slightly more than this as compared with the British mutineers. In other words, the first-born hybrid generation showed an increase of about 2½ inches in stature. Their reproductive rate was one of the highest I was able to find in the records—11.4 children per mating. The succeeding generations have suffered some decline from these figures, and this too conforms to the experience with hybridization in plants and animals. Although the crossing of independent human genetic strains has not always produced results equivalent to the Pitcairn situation, enough parallels to it have been recorded to suggest strongly that hybrid vigor may and does occur in human crosses.

The relevance of this phenomenon to the increasing bulk and size of western European and American populations seems convincing when we compare settlement and breeding patterns before and after the onset of the Industrial Age in Europe and examine the comparable effects that developed from the migration history of the United States. In the Middle Ages the population in western Europe had become firmly stabilized under a feudal system. People lived in small communities, often isolated from one another, and with mobility extremely limited, not only by a social and economic system that provided little or no inducement for relocation, but also, for the mass of the people, by the lack of a mode of transportation except their own legs. These enclaves tended under the circumstances to become, in effect, isolated breeding units. A young man looking for a wife would be unlikely to go very far afield for one, not more than a few miles. If his marriage were arranged by his family, the choice would most likely be a neighbor. Even today in India, where most of the people live in small villages and lack means of transport, these geographic limitations in breeding patterns have been observed and recorded.

Such conditions obviously and inevitably led to inbreeding and genetic differentiation within the national population. A recent study of such ancient population enclaves in one small area of a valley in Italy revealed that in the course of some generations of inbreeding distinct genetic differences had accumulated in the various groups that differentiated one from another. This rise of distinct strains within a single population would appear then to be a normal result of isolation. Effects frequently observed in such inbred communities are a decrease in size (a result paralleled

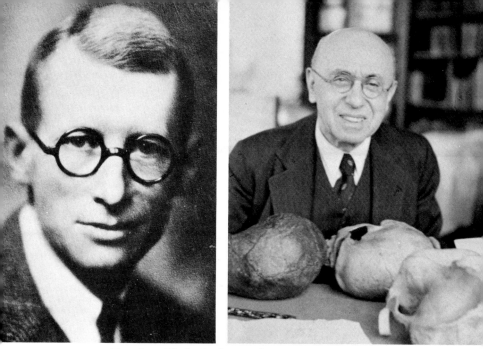

ABOVE LEFT, Davidson Black, Professor of Anatomy at Peking Union Medical College, the first to recognize the identity of Peking man.

ABOVE RIGHT, Franz Weidenreich, the distinguished anatomist and anthropologist who made the definitive study of Peking man.

BELOW, Camp Holcomb, U.S. Marine base where the fossils of Peking man were sent for shipment to the United States in 1941.

Panoramic view of Chou Kou Tien, the site of the discovery of Peking man.

Close-up of Chou Kou Tien.

ABOVE, Rope enclosure at right outlines area where the first and second skulls of Peking man were found.

RIGHT, Excavation at Chou Kou Tien revealing the depth of the deposit.

BELOW, These are the last stages in the removal of the fossil known as Skull 3.

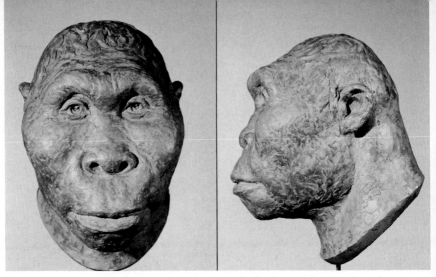

Zinjanthropus, one of the *Australopithecines*. Early Pleistocene from East Africa. Restoration by author.

RESTORATION OF HEADS
REPRESENTING VARIOUS STAGES OF HOMINID EVOLUTION

Pithecanthropus erectus. Mid-Pleistocene from Java. Restoration by author.

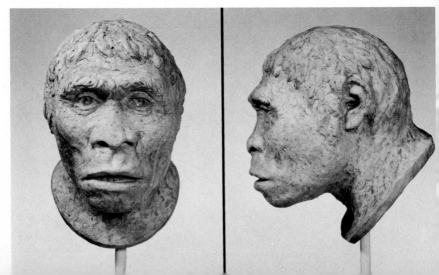

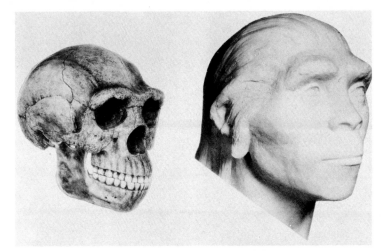

ABOVE, Female *Sinanthropus pekinensis*. Mid-Pleistocene from China. Restoration by Franz Weidenreich.

RIGHT AND BELOW, *Male Sinanthropus pekinensis*. Mid-Pleistocene, from the Peking population, China. Restoration by the author.

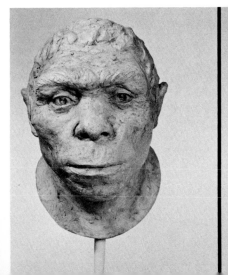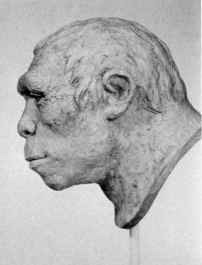

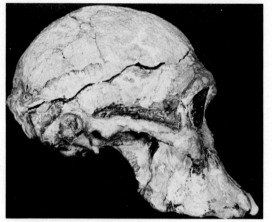

Australopithecus africanus.

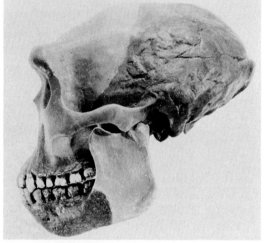

Pithecanthropus erectus Number 4.

Sinanthropus pekinensis Number 3.

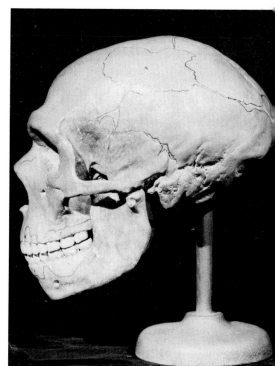

RIGHT, Neanderthal man.

BELOW, *Female Sinanthropus* (center) compared with a female gorilla (right) and a modern Chinese (left).

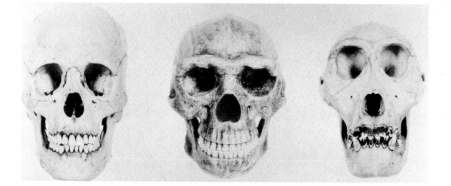

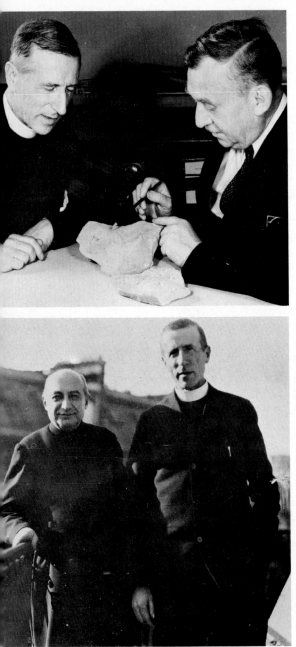

LEFT, Père Teilhard de Chardin (at left) with geologist Walter Granger, studying a specimen.

BELOW LEFT, Abbé Breuil (at left) with Père Teilhard de Chardin, active participants in the study of the remains of Peking man.

BELOW, The "War Booty" brought back from China by an American soldier, whose widow alleges that these are some of the "lost" fossils of Peking man.

THE GREEK HERITAGE FOUNDATION

in much experimental data on animals) and an increase in genetic defects. The first, I saw illustrated very vividly in a community in Italy that I visited some years ago. For centuries this village, Settifrati—the last one on a road east of Rome before the ascent to the uninhabited mountains—had been virtually cut off from contact with its neighbors. Until a few years before my visit, the only access to the village was a donkey trail. As a result, the families that made up the community were highly inbred, and there were only about a half-dozen patronymics, or family names, for a population that had once numbered well over a thousand. One characteristic of the villagers that struck me immediately was their short stature, distinctly below the standards of the same ethnic group living in the less isolated villages in the area.

There have been a number of studies on such inbred communities, including some in the remote mountainous areas of Japan, that support the conclusion that inbreeding tends to reduce stature and thus accounts for the small size of Medieval European populations.

Along with decreased physical size, such inbred communities also show a greater frequency of mental and physiological defects. A lowering of mental ability and an increase in genetic disorders in hearing have been reported for such groups in New England and in Switzerland. A relatively rare recessive disorder may not show itself to any significant degree in the usual outbred community, but where inbreeding is the common practice it is far more likely to become a serious phenomenon. This has happened on the island of Tristan da Cunha, where a small population has been inbreeding since the early nineteenth century and its continued existence is now threatened by a genetic pathology.

The existence of distinct genetic strains or populations within a nation may also, as is well known, result from repeated invasions. Pockets of indigenous groups, retreating before the invaders or thrust by them into refuge areas, often survive for centuries or even millennia. The Welsh and

Gaelic groups in Scotland represent such strains that were never absorbed into the general population. Similar surviving lines are common in Europe as well: the Basques, Bretons, Walloons and the Flamands to name only a few. Thus isolation and tribal history produced a patchwork of distinct genetic lines which would interbreed when the flow from these various communities began to inundate the industrial centers that burgeoned in England in the eighteenth century and somewhat later on the Continent. Country folk who for generations had maintained a considerable degree of isolation were now in contact with other strains in their new environment. Heterosis, or hybrid vigor, resulted from such a mingling.

In the United States, strains from various sections of Great Britain which at home might never have encountered each other now were in close contact, and consequently the intermingling that only became common in England in the eighteenth and nineteenth centuries began in the American colonies in the early seventeenth century. To this, of course, was added the stream of European immigrants, whose linkages with most of the British population had been severed for several millenia.

This theory can be corroborated by looking at the Japanese, who have shown a decidedly similar consequence since the start of their Industrial Age. For centuries they, too, had a geographically highly stabilized population, with many of the settlements inbred as in medieval Europe. They were, by and large, a distinctly short people. The very marked increment in size of the young generation today can be dated to the modern industrialization that, beginning in the 1920's, brought about a major population reshuffling and a consequent intermingling of the genetic lines that had developed in the centuries before. It is, I suggest, significant that no sign of this change appeared in Japan while the phenomenon was well under way in Europe, and that its occurrence in Japan almost 200 years later is timed to the same onset of industrial reshuffling as in Europe.

I have discussed fluctuations in body size of recent as well as ancient man to clarify the position that Peking man occupies, not only in relation to his precursors, but to his successors as well. It is evident, I think, that the recent increments in size that various industrial populations have displayed are not part of a permanent evolutionary trend. They have been too rapid to reflect such a tendency, and they are more typical of ephemeral conditions, both genetic and environmental. This, however, does not deny the sure, steady and far more extensive evolutionary modification in the hominid line that is clearly evident in the fossil record of several million years. In this context, we can trace a progressively upward curve, allowing for minor fluctuations attributable to other factors. Thus, Peking man can be said to have reached the bottom rung of *Homo sapiens* variation in his size and stature.

Before turning to Peking man's facial appearance, it is possible to derive from the fossil bones several other of his bodily characteristics. It is clear from the lengths of the femur and the humerus that the proportion of the arm to the leg was considerably greater than we find in present-day man, reflecting a more primitive condition. The basic trait characteristic of the hominid line is upright posture and erect gait. Indeed, evidence of this in the fossil remains is one of the indisputable criteria of hominid affiliation. One requirement necessary to enable the emergent hominids to manage with skill and efficiency in their new ground-centered environment was a relative increase in leg length. Parallel to this change came a shortening of the arm, which no longer functioned in locomotion. Thus a gradual shift is observable in the course of human evolution, with modern man showing the shortest arms relative to leg length, or, to put it another way, showing the longest legs relative to arm and body length. In the gorilla, the proportion of the humeral length to the femoral is 117.0, and in the chimpanzee it is about 101.0. In modern Chinese the leg has become so much longer and the arm shorter in relation to each other that this index is consequently reduced to 70.0–71.0. In Peking man it is 79.3, according to Weidenreich.

Among the few skeletal fragments of Peking man, an almost complete collarbone was also unearthed. Its structure was fairly robust and in no way significantly different from ours, but its length enables one to estimate the shoulder width, which, considering the size of Peking man, must have been fairly broad.

From all this evidence we can envisage a body quite short in height, but muscular and broad-shouldered, with rather short legs and long arms that reached rather closer to the knees than do ours.

But it is the face that generally attracts our major interest when we encounter a stranger. Many of us even go so far as to draw conclusions as to his character and personality from the facial and cranial features he displays. Although phrenology is no longer given the serious attention it enjoyed in the early nineteenth century, when the vogue was at its height, its subtle effects still linger. A well-known British novelist has related how his and his brother's futures were determined by phrenological assessments that his father had ordered. It was on the basis of this diagnosis that he was considered suited for a higher education and sent to the university.

But even though phrenology has virtually lost its former authority, physiognomical guidelines have retained a common acceptance. Even today, novelists speak of a strong, projecting chin as indicative of strength of character, and of a high, wide brow as betokening a lofty intellect. We have all read of the thick sensual lips that could be a warning or an invitation. And who would trust anyone with eyes set close together, or not trust one whose eyes are wide-set?

If we used these criteria, Peking man would, I am afraid, be ranked below his deserts. He had no chin as we think of one, and his brow was decidedly low. Moreover, his skull was by our standards relatively small and distinctly flattened down. We would have trusted him, however, for his eyes were set well apart.

What we generally think of as the chin is the projecting lower segment of the mandible, but technically the whole anterior portion of the lower jaw constitutes this feature. We are naturally so accustomed to seeing the forward projection of this lower segment that we think of someone as chinless if he lacks this characteristic. But the "chin," in human evolution, is a recent acquisition. The immediate predecessor of *Homo sapiens*, Neanderthal man, who lived in Europe up to about 45,000 years ago, frequently shows no jutting "chin," although in a few cases one can detect the beginnings of one. The more primitive forms of man were universally chinless, with a slight backward and downward slope from the roots of the teeth. This shape, more or less exaggerated, is standard for all primates and indeed for all mammals and is functionally linked with a projecting snout. But in the hominids, beginning early in their career, the dentition began to change. The large projecting canines of their ancestors underwent a massive reduction in size, and the gap in the row of teeth that permitted the upper and lower canines to interlock in occlusion closed up as the forward teeth shrank back. The teeth in general became smaller. The molars, which had formerly increased noticeably in size from the first to the third, now began to undergo a marked modification with the progression in reverse. Clearly, the dental function was being affected by man's adaptation to ground living and a change in diet, and possibly the hand taking over some of the former functions of the teeth also played a role. Though experts debate these matters, they all recognize the incontrovertible changes.

This decline in masticatory power and vigor was reflected in the shrinkage of the jaw. From being a markedly protrusive feature of a face that jutted well forward of the brow, it gradually receded until, with us, it forms part of a face that is positioned more or less under the brow.

This retreat and refinement of the jaw in turn left it exposed to muscular tensions that had previously been counteracted by the robusticity of the jawbone itself and, in the ape jaw, where the muscular power was even greater, by a kind of horizontal strut on the inner side of the chin, known as the "simian shelf." One set of muscles, the internal pterygoids, exerts a tension which has increased as the jaw retreated, largely because of the resulting alteration in the relationship and angulation of muscle to bone. This in turn led to a thickening of the chin area where the right and left segments of the mandible join. Instead of an interior shelf like that of the apes, however, the reinforcement developed on the lower external surface, for a simian shelf in man's markedly reduced jaw would have left a totally inadequate space for the tongue. In Peking man this thickening process was, of course, well along, but it had not yet reached the stage where a chin could be seen.

This retreat of the face had another effect that has made the human face distinctive, if not unique as in the case of the chin. The nose, which in the apes is almost flat with a scarcely discernible bridge, has become in *Homo sapiens* a highly notable feature. Its size, curve and flare are noticed and evaluated, but not always by the same standards since various cultures and populations tend to set up their own esthetic criteria. It is perhaps fortunate that most European and American tourists in China, Africa and Polynesia—to mention only a few areas—don't know the native languages well enough to appreciate the comments their nasal distinction elicits from the less-favored or differently endowed. I well remember the comments of a Polynesian friend on the peculiar nasal architecture of the Europeans he had studied with astonishment. The "aristocratic" nose of a Virginia Woolf would have called for a different adjective in his judgment.

Just as the chin was a consequence of the reduction of the face and mandible in the course of human evolution, so the typically prominent nose of *Homo sapiens* can be seen as a result of the same process. But the dynamics are somewhat different. Whereas the lower jaw was part of the reduction process, with the chin developing as a secondary response to the resulting muscular stress, the nose is a kind of mesa that has retained its size while the surrounding facial structure has eroded. Since the function of the nose and its chambers has remained intact, its bony housing could not be diminished as the face retreated. The inevitable result was, of course, the increasingly visible prominence of its structure, not through growth so much as by the retention of its basic size.

In Peking man the nose has taken on some prominence as compared with the early hominids and the apes, although by European standards it would be described as low and relatively broad. Nevertheless, it is a feature that we would recognize as distinctly human and well within the range of modern man.

As one might deduce from the dependence of a prominent nose and a jutting chin upon the shrinkage of the face, the fact that Peking man has no chin and only a low nasal elevation suggests that his face had not retreated as drastically as modern man's. In profile, his face projected forward and would technically be called prognathic. But compared with the projecting faces of the apes or even such early hominids as the *Australopithecines*, the facial protrusion of Peking man was slight.

The width of his face was also notable, largely due to the prominence of the cheekbones. Weidenreich, in his detailed study of the crania, refers to this characteristic as one of a series that is highly suggestive of modern Mongoloid people.

Among Peking man's visible features, perhaps none was more distinctive than the size and formation of his skull. First and most striking was the massive projection of the brow just above the eyes. This was due to the strong development of the supraorbital torus—a horizontal bar of bone extending the full width of the lower margin of the forehead.

This torus is called a primitive characteristic since it is highly developed in man's earliest ancestors and is also a special feature of the anthropoid apes. But whereas in Peking man's predecessors this jutting brow slopes backward and upward at a very low angle, in Peking man himself the expansion of the brain has developed a slight bulge that rises at a steeper pitch immediately back of the brow, giving him rather more of a forehead.

The size of the brain is notably greater in Peking man than in the *Australopithecines* or even his relative, Java man. On the average it is 1075 c.c., which is approximately twice the magnitude of the early hominids. Compared with modern man, it falls short of any living group by 200–300 c.c. Thus, by our standards, Peking man would have looked small-headed. And if his hair did not conceal the shape of his head, we would have noticed its peculiar form. The skull was relatively flat, with its greatest width just above the ears. The side walls sloped inward and upward in a double plane, producing an effect like a gambrel roof. A pronounced ridge extended lengthwise along the middle of the crown, and a strong bony ridge projected backward just above the nape of the neck. This last feature partly reflects the presence of a powerful set of neck muscles that served to balance the head on the vertebral column. It suggests that Peking man had a somewhat bull-like neck, with the muscles riding high on the occiput and concealing the rounded projection which is common in modern man.

If Weidenreich were correct in his interpretation of a number of dental, skeletal and cranial features, one might have recognized the living Peking man on first viewing as being of Mongoloid origin. In an impressive number of these features Weidenreich found characteristics that are especially typical of modern Chinese and related strains. To take one example: The "shovel-shaped" incisor is a tooth that has a kind of thickening along its lateral edges that gives it a vague resemblance to the old-fashioned coal shovel. It is very frequently found in the Chinese today, as well as in other Mongoloid populations. Even the American Indians, who are related to the Mongoloid strain, share this characteristic, and the Polynesians, who are very probably part Mongoloid in origin, also display it in lesser frequency. In non-Mongoloid peoples, such as Europeans and Africans, it occurs quite infrequently. The fact that Peking man also possesses this type of front tooth becomes, under the circumstances, highly suggestive.

If this similarity with present-day Mongoloid characteristics, however, were the only one, it might be discounted on various grounds. But Weidenreich found other traits among the *Sinanthropines* that are especially characteristic of living Mongoloid people and absent or rare in others. He lists, among others, a flattening of the shaft of the femur, known as platymeria; the shape, contours and angulation of the nasal bones; the architectural details of the cheekbones; the high frequency of bony exostoses, or outgrowths, in the upper jaw and in the bony ear; and the notably frequent occurrence of the so-called "Inca bones" found in the occipital area of the skull. He summed up the results of these comparisons by asserting that they corroborate

> ... first the thesis that *Sinanthropus* is a direct ancestor of *Homo sapiens*, and secondly that there is a closer relationship to Mongols—or at least to certain Mongolian groups—than to any other races, particularly to whites. In any case, it is safe to say that racial groups supplied with those peculiarities have *Sinanthropus* in their ancestry. Had only one character been transmitted, the relationship might be questioned, but as there are *twelve* special features, which behave in the same way, the coincidence cannot be accidental.

That the living Chinese tend to regard Peking man as at least one of their ancestors would be strongly justified by these comparisons. That Peking man looked like a primitive version of the present-day Chinese would seem to be equally borne out by the available data.

4

HOW HE LIVED

How the men and women in the Peking area lived 500,000 years ago can only be inferred from the archaeological traces of their activities and from what we can observe today of primitive hunting–gathering peoples. It has also been suggested that the behavior of primates can throw considerable light on the social organization of primitive man; but this has been strongly questioned by George B. Schaller and Gordon Lowther, who point out the wide discrepancies that exist between closely related primate groups. These differences can easily arise from various ways of adapting to ecological conditions. Schaller and Lowther, on the contrary, see value in comparing nonprimate carnivores with early man since both are hunting animals. But on the whole, since *Sinanthropus* is much closer to living man in his physical, intellectual and cultural evolution than he is to any primitive hominid or primate, the simple hunting–gathering groups of today are more reliable guides. Even though drawing parallels between simple cultures of our time and those of half a million years ago can be misleading, it can, if done with caution, provide valuable insights. For example, the bow and arrow, which can make a significant difference in the amount of food that can be secured in a given area, was widely used by recent hunting folk but unknown to Peking man. Yet, as I shall discuss later, the relation between population size and ecology among modern hunter–gatherers can give us valid clues as to the size of the Peking community.

In certain respects, the Peking population lived off the land in a way not very different from present-day hunting-gathering people as far as simple food-collecting is concerned. They gathered the natural produce of the country and hunted its wild denizens for meat. Long before cultivated plants were developed and used in agriculture, men and women, probably the latter more frequently, garnered whatever plant foods were indigenous to their locality. We know that seeds, fruits and nuts must have been mainstays of their diet from the botanical identification of undigested seed in fossil feces and from traces of other wild produce in the debris of their ancient living areas.

It is hard for us, so accustomed to the harvesting of highly selected, planted crops, to realize that most if not all of them do not exist under natural conditions, and that the original plants from which our wheat, rice, corn and barley are derived yielded far less than the developed strains. The highly complex and artificial conditions of modern agricultural technology, with its bountiful harvests in highly concentrated areas, began only some 10,000 to 12,000 years ago. Before that time, the precursors of these and other food plants were thinly scattered over large areas, demanding of their collectors an intimate knowledge of the countryside. Sometimes they had to be prepared to spend long hours for a meager harvest. Before the development of agriculture all people, except for those living under difficult conditions, like the Eskimo in the Arctic, depended considerably on gathering these wild fruits and seeds. And the Eskimo also, for a brief season in midsummer, seek out wild fruit as a welcome addition to their diet. Even in the desert areas of Australia the aborigines are able to find and use a surprising variety of native plants adapted to these adverse conditions. In temperate areas, where the winters made edible plants seasonal, their availability was limited except where storage techniques had been developed to allow some extension of their use. Whether the *Sinanthropines* were able to achieve this is not known.

In modern hunting–gathering societies the women frequently go off in groups, with their younger children helping. Since gathering wild seeds, fruits or roots even under favorable conditions is time-consuming and the pickings are usually adequate for only a day or so, it must have been a regular daily chore that took up perhaps as much as a morning. It is, I think, reasonable to assume that the *Sinanthropine* women also made something of a social event of their food gathering as they went off in groups accompanied by their young, who inevitably would have provided diversion, play and occasionally the need for parental control and discipline.

What these women used as containers for their harvest is unknown. It is improbable in the light of their more advanced cultural and technological development that they simply ate as they gathered, the way primates do and very likely as the early hominids also did. Something was required as they worked their way through woods and fields hour after hour if their hands were to be free for picking. Since they knew nothing of pottery and probably no more of basketry, my own guess is that the only possibilities available to them would have been wild gourds if any of sufficient size grew in the neighborhood, large tough leaves that could be pinned together with twigs or spines, wooden bowls that their stone and bone tools would have been adequate to shape and hollow out from fallen trees, or bags of skin or leather. Although the last may seem too complicated an artifact for so primitive a culture, it is reasonable, I suspect, to infer that they knew something of the technique of preparing and using the skins of wild animals. After all, they were living in a far from tropical region and they could scarcely have survived the rigors of even relatively mild winters without some kind of garments to cover their shivering nakedness since they had no insulating body cover, like the dense fur of other mammals, nor a thick, fatty subdermal layer that might have served the same purpose. Since the art of weaving was not developed until hundreds of thousands of years later, the only available natural sources of body covering would have been bark, reeds or grasses and skins, and the first two would scarcely have been the answer. In fact, the discovery of animal skins as a means of conserving body heat in cold weather may well have been the critical factor in early man's ability to move into the temperate and cooler areas of the Old World, for those who originated in tropical or semitropical areas were covered, at most, with a relatively thin growth of hair that provided little protection against the cold. This then represents one more example of the way in which man in his evolution has increasingly adapted to the natural environment through technology rather than by physiological or anatomical changes.

How such skins might have been prepared and fashioned into garments is a matter of conjecture since, like the flesh of their wearers, they would have rotted away long ago and left no trace of their manufacture or use. If they had been cut and sewn into fitted garments, we would expect to find the cutting tools and needles to accomplish the task. But even the absence of such implements need not eliminate the possibility that skins were used, for they could simply have been draped on the body. Thus, if animal skins were a necessity for these early men to survive in a cold climate, the material for containers on collecting expeditions would have been at hand.

We are apt to consider the decorative value of clothing as much, if not more, than its utility. There are many tropical areas where virtually no clothing whatever is actually needed or worn, yet trinkets, necklaces, rings, hair ornaments, waistbands and a variety of other purely decorative elements are treasured and used. When this distinctly human concern with the esthetic enrichment of the body became established no one knows. Whether Peking men and women used clothing purely for bodily protection or for decoration as well we cannot deduce from any tangible evidence. My own guess is that they had advanced so far in the course of human evolution that a practice as fundamental and widespread as decorative enhancement must already have surfaced, if only in a primitive form.

To return to the process of food-gathering, the only other abundant source of nutriment is the flesh of beast, bird, fish and other animals. For an inland people like the Peking population, the rich aquatic life of the seashore would not have played a major role, although some fish would have been available in nearby streams.

When we examine the fossilized bones in the debris of the caves of Chou Kou Tien in order to determine what animals Peking man actually hunted and consumed, we find a considerable assortment of mammals, birds, fish, toads, frogs and turtles. Not all of these had been eaten by the *Sinanthropines*. Some, like the hyænas and cave bears, may have died there naturally, since they too had been occupants of the caves, for Peking man did not live there uninterruptedly during the hundreds or thousands of years that he made use of them. At times he might have left on nomadic forays and for considerable periods apparently abandoned the caves altogether.

Aside from the remains of nonhuman occupants, some of the osseous debris could have been brought in by the animals inhabiting the caves. Hyænas, for example, are notorious scavengers and would have dragged their prey in where they could feast in relative peace. Some animals might have wandered in for one reason or another and died there. The numerous bird bones found were more likely a result of the human kill since, on the whole, birds are more difficult for animals to capture.

One important clue in trying to reconstruct the *Sinanthropine* diet is whether or not the bony remains of edible animals show signs of having been roasted. The bones that have been roasted in fire must have been carried to the caves by men, for a fire would have driven away hyænas and cave bears, not attracted them. Thus, it can be concluded without much doubt that most if not all of the charred bones were burned by Peking man. The Abbé Breuil, who made a careful study of these bones, decided on the basis of considerable knowledge of such archeological evidence that many of them had been burnt when fresh. The antlers of deer and the horns of other animals displayed similar evidence of having been burned in a freshly killed state. Some of this roasting was apparently part of the technique these early men used in preparing their tools. But it is, I think, a reasonable inference that some of the burnt bones that were not used for artifacts simply represent the remains of animals roasted for food. Long before the *Sinanthropines* appeared, man had become carnivorous. In the early stages of hominid evolution, he ate his animal prey raw. But the fire available to Peking man opened a new dimension in his cuisine that he could scarcely avoid, and one that it is inconceivable that he would have abandoned once he had become aware of its enhancement of his diet.

The presence of fish, frogs and turtles in the deposits has been accounted for by M. N. Bien of the Cenozoic Research Laboratory, who studied their remains, as a result of the nearby river's flooding the interior of the caves and leaving them behind. He even admits the possibility suggested by Teilhard de Chardin and C. C. Young, that they were brought into the caves by animals. But nothing is said of the possibility that Peking man also might have deposited them there, as part of his haul. In my opinion it is unreasonable to conclude that a hominid with so developed a brain as Peking man had, with the clearly documented capacity to use and control fire and to manipulate stone and bone for his technology, would have been unable to capture these animals and use them for food.

If gathering seeds and fruits is a process readily accessible to any primate whose grasping hand and opposable thumb would make plucking such food an easy function, the hunting and catching of wild game is another matter. The early hominids had not evolved from a carnivorous line nicely equipped with claws and teeth to grapple with and kill their prey, which they could stalk and seize by their bursts of high speed and leaps. Nor, as two-legged, erect creatures, could they hope to overtake any of the fast running game, such as deer and goats. Even such small prey as rabbits or mice are not easy to catch by hand alone. Fish would also present a problem. But frogs or insects, which children today can catch with ease, would have posed no difficulty.

The question, however, that is difficult to answer from any archeological evidence is how Peking man did his hunting. He had no bow and arrow. We are reduced here to pure guesswork. We envisage his using rocks to hit and maim animals that he might have approached stealthily. He might have used the sharp points of antlers and horns that the Abbé Breuil described as having been carefully fashioned to provide a convenient grip. It would have required a skill and dexterity that cannot be denied to this prehistoric Chinese population.

That they had a notable manual skill is apparent in the stone and bone tools that survive them. Any wooden implements, which it seems most likely they used, would have disintegrated long before the remains of their makers were discovered. The stone tools now are the most abundant and are found throughout the layers of sediment and debris that fill the caves and which contain the actual remains of the *Sinanthropines* themselves. This association can only imply that they were fashioned by Peking man.

Although this conclusion is now universally accepted, there were once some dissident opinions. M. Boule and other experts appraised the situation back in the 1930's, when this evidence was coming to light. They were of the opinion that *Sinanthropus* was too primitive a hominid to have been capable of a stone technology of the sophistication these tools displayed. They offered instead the theory that another, higher contemporaneous form of man made the stone tools and used them, in part, against his inferior neighbors—namely, these *Sinanthropines*. Not only has there never been any evidence that such a superior population coexisted with Peking man, but, had there been one, Peking man would have borrowed its techniques and used them for his own purposes. In the cultural history of man the contact between different peoples with different cultures has usually, if the distinctions were not too great, led to borrowing and the diffusion of ideas and techniques.

The stones that Peking man employed for his tools consisted mainly of green sandstone and quartz of two kinds (vein and quartzite), and a few of chert and limestone. The vein quartz and green sandstone could have been found in a nearby stream. The quartzite, however, would have required visits to granite massifs some few miles to the northeast and to the south of the caves. For a hunting–gathering people this would not have been an unusual distance to travel for essential supplies.

The stone tools themselves can be conveniently classified into a number of broad categories. First, there are many rather rude and fairly large, roughly flaked boulders or choppers. Some of these also show a shaping of the butt end for a hand grip. The most common type of tool found from top to bottom of the layers was the quartz core with flaking on both sides to give it a cutting edge. Almost as numerous was a flake tool which appears to have been made and used more frequently in the later occupation periods. This type was chipped mainly from quartz and quartzite cores and came in various shapes, some rather elongated. Père Teilhard de Chardin, who examined and reported on these stone tools, also noted some rostrate, or keeled, forms with a kind of beak that was probably used as a burin or chisel. He also observed that some had been flaked and shaped to provide a distinct point that would have been effective as a borer. Finally, in his classification he set aside as a distinct type a number of limestone pieces, some of which had been metamorphosed, that were apparently hammering stones. In addition to these, The Abbé Breuil, in his publication on the tools, observed a few additional forms. On the whole, he noted a general resemblance to the stone artifacts known from the early Paleolithic of Europe, but he stressed the fact that the Chou Kou Tien assemblage had a distinctive character of its own, which implies an independent tradition. Nowadays, archaeologists place the *Sinanthropine* stone technology in the chopper–chopping tradition that developed in Southeast Asia, including China, and thus differentiate it from the emergent style of stone technique found in Europe and Africa. This would, of course, suggest that the *Sinanthropine* population had been pretty much isolated from European or African influence.

Although such tools as these are by our standards very crude indeed, they could nevertheless serve the *Sinanthropines* for a number of functions, such as cutting, piercing, scraping and pounding or hammering, that they would not have been able to perform without them, unless they happened to find natural stones suited to the purposes, and this would have been rare. Had they been common and easily available, man would not have found it necessary to develop the primitive stone technology that lies at the base of all the remarkable developments which make up the world we live in today.

Along with these stone tools, a fair assemblage of bone instruments has also survived, including antlers and horns that must have been used as piercing tools. In addition, some of the fresh bones had been exposed to fire to crack them into longitudinal pieces that could then be shaped at one end for various purposes.

When anyone without a special knowledge of the skill that goes into chipping and flaking stone tools looks at an assemblage of them such as was found at Chou Kou Tien, he is apt to regard them as extremely crude, neither worthy of any great intelligence nor indicative of a high level of ability. If, however, such an observer tries to duplicate them, it is unlikely that he will be able to approach, let alone duplicate, their special qualities. Stonework of this kind requires a knowledge of the way natural, rough specimens can be fractured and shaped, how and where to exert the pressures that will remove the stone bit by bit until the model in mind takes shape. I well remember a few years ago when Mr. Donald Crabtree, an expert knapper, demonstrated to a group of archaeological experts the chipping and flaking techniques he had acquired. Now that the knappers in England have become virtually extinct, he is one of the few living men who have such a knowledge. It was astonishing to see with what apparent ease and obvious skill he was able to extract from a rough stone a beautifully shaped and efficient tool that the rest of us could scarcely have approached even though some of his observers were professionally acquainted with the theory of stone-flaking. This kind of handiwork, used by *Sinanthropines*, represented a long tradition and a comparatively high level of intelligence. Its crudity compared with modern machinery should not be taken to define the relative abilities of these prehistoric men.

One other source of food available to the Peking men, where some of them might have been the losers rather than the gainers, requires some comment. The possibility was suggested by some scholars shortly after the fossils were first discovered that they represented the debris of cannibalistic feasts. The fact that none of the skulls was intact but all were, in fact, badly shattered and fragmented might at first glance support the idea. Moreover, cannibalism is not unknown even among living or recently living peoples. The Marquesans, for example, were known to have eaten enemies slain in combat. Melville, in *Typee*, described in some detail the ceremonies connected with this ritual, which he observed while living with the inhabitants of Taipivai. The tradition was still alive in 1929 when, on my first visit to the Marquesas, I talked with an old man, the son of a former chief in Taiohae, a valley near Melville's "Typee." He told me that he had in his childhood eaten human flesh, and had been given a particularly delicious joint because of his filial relation to the chief. Cannibalism was also practised in New Zealand, in Borneo and in various parts of Africa, and even Herodotus speaks of "anthropophagi," or man-eaters, who were reputed to have followed this custom in the outlying regions of the Hellenic world. Perhaps nowhere at any time did the custom become as inflated as it did among the Aztecs. On special occasions they slew thousands of victims, who were offered to the gods on their temples. The flesh and various organs were then ritually eaten to enhance the powers of the slaughterers. The implication, of course, is that cannibalism in these areas where it was a regular phenomenon was considered a normal source of meat. Actually, when the circumstances are known, cannibalism was never common or accepted simply as a source of food. Its practice was usually associated with a distinct ritualism that had mystical overtones and was not an excuse for a gourmet dinner. When we examine man's primate relatives or even other orders of mammals, we find that cannibalism, or the eating of members of one's own species, is never a regular practice. Under dire stress such behavior may occur, as it is known to have occurred among humans, but except for its ritualistic performance it has no established tradition as a source of food.

All this argues against cannibalism as a normal source of food for the Peking population. Nor can one make a substantial case for the possibility that ritualistic cannibalism existed at Chou Kou Tien 500,000 years ago. The fact that the skulls and skeletons are broken and fragmented is more realistically explained as the result of crushing by the weight of the rocks and layers of debris falling upon the bones from the ceilings of the caves. It is, in fact, very rare to find fossils as old as these to be complete and in good condition.

One of the most human of all human abilities is the capacity to use a spoken language. That is not to say that other animals do not communicate with each other and even with different species. The sounds that dolphins use, the songs of birds, the groans, grunts, whistles, barks, growls and even the gestures that are made by many birds, mammals, reptiles, amphibia, fishes and insects have meaning and carry messages. But language, with an almost infinite variety of words that carry direct as well as abstract meaning, is unique to man. The world we live in is inconceivable without it.

It is natural, therefore, to wonder and speculate about the language Peking man used. Or, to put it another way, did he use language as we know it? This, of course, raises the question of why and when man in his evolution acquired this remarkable ability. If we look to the fossil record for answers, we will be disappointed for the obvious reason that a nonmaterial phenomenon such as this can leave no physical trace of its existence. Only when language had become embodied in writing could it be recorded for preservation, and this did not occur until about 5,500 to 6,000 years ago, when formalized and systematic writing became a necessity for the emergent and increasingly complex civilizations that first appeared in the Near East and Egypt. For an unknown length of time before that, however, some form of language must have been used. It is, of course, possible to see in some of the Neolithic cave and rock paintings and incisions on bone some gropings in the direction of a graphic representation of a spoken language. The dating of these grafitti may add another four or five thousand years to the history of writing—unless we extend such initial efforts still further back to the latter part of the Paleolithic and its transition into the Mesolithic, when bone and ivory relics were incised with markings that Alexander Marshack has suggested are numerical recordings. The famous cave paintings of the Upper Paleolithic in France and Spain, although they exhibit an extraordinary esthetic sense, do not reveal any effort at symbolic writing or notation.

When we look elsewhere for clues, we have little to go on except for some negative inferences. One of these, based on neurological, anatomical and phylogenetic comparisons, is that the earliest hominids were probably not yet endowed with a linguistic capability that we would unquestionably characterize as language. The ability to talk is considered to be at least in part the effect of the increasing complexity of the brain and of the interrelationship of its various centers.

Some arguments have also been made that articulate speech, with its highly complex patterns of sound, became possible only as the result of anatomical changes in the larynx and in the sound chambers of the mouth and nose, which lie above it. These were produced in part by the retraction of the face and jaw in the course of human evolution.

When we examine the evidence provided by our closest living primate relatives, none of them turns out to use speech as we know it. Sounds, gestures and facial expressions carry messages, but words are not used. That they are capable of some very elementary forms of speech seems unquestionable since in a few experimental cases, a chimpanzee or an orang can be taught to understand a few simple words. And in one case at least, a chimpanzee, Viki, was with great effort taught to enunciate "mama," "papa" and "cup" by her mentors, the psychologists K. J. and C. Hayes. In actual speech this is about the best that any ape has been able to achieve. More recently, R. A. and B. T. Gardner, another psychological team, have explored the potentialities of chimpanzee communication patterns, and have had remarkable success in training their chimpanzee, Washoe, to comprehend nonvocal signs and symbols of a surprising variety. The latest count I have seen was over 100, and since Washoe is apparently very adept at this kind of communication, the number by now may be appreciably greater.

The earliest hominids whose brain size can be estimated were the *Australopithecines* and *Homo habilis* of Africa. The former had a brain size roughly the same as the gorilla and about 100–150 c.c. larger than the chimpanzee. *Homo habilis*, however, exceeded the *Australopithecines*, reaching a cranial capacity of slightly over 600 c.c. This crude comparison suggests that size alone is a measure of the intellectual capacity of the brain. Although highly important, we know it is not the only factor. If, however, allowance is made for the fact that gross brain size is correlated to some degree with body size, then these hominids would have to be ranked well above the gorilla, whose body bulk was certainly considerably greater than that of *Australopithecus*. Phillip V. Tobias has arrived at a more accurate comparison basing his estimates on the Jerison equation, which attempts to measure "extra" neurons—those beyond the basic needs of the body, which are available for adaptive mechanisms—hence intelligence. According to these calculations, the chimpanzee possesses 3.4 billion extra neurons, the gorilla 3.5 billions and the *Australopithecines* 3.9 to 4.5 billions. Although it is apparent from these figures that the *Australopithecines* had made some progress beyond the ape level, they were still far short of that attained by *Homo sapiens*, which Tobias estimates to range from 8.4 to 8.9 billion extra neurons.

If these primates in their natural condition did not use language, and if language is, to an important degree, dependent upon neurological development, it would seem unlikely that our early hominid predecessors the *Australopithecines* would have been capable of employing it. Moreover, if the anatomical requirements for speech have any validity, these early manlike creatures would not have been properly or adequately equipped to make the sounds that are an integral and necessary part of language.

Most students of human evolution take this conclusion for granted and so the *Australopithecines*, one of the earliest known hominids, dating as far back as one to four million years, have been eliminated as the pioneers in this distinctly human activity. To the question of when man did acquire this ability, the answer at present can only be—we don't know. If I were to indulge in further speculation, I might look for insights in the recapitulation theory, which states that man, as well as other animals, tends in a general way to develop through stages that repeat or suggest earlier phases

of his evolution. Although it has been abundantly demonstrated that this theory cannot be taken too literally, there
remain a number of sequential events that cannot be so readily dismissed. I would suggest that the developing child,
who only begins to use language in a tentative way between
one and two years of age, when his brain is at about the 900
c.c. level, may give us a clue. Recognizing the many individual variations, this may neverthless indicate that it is only
when a child reaches this level in the development of the
brain that he becomes able to respond to verbal stimuli and
reproduce it with sophistication. Using the theory of recapitulation, we might deduce that *Pithecanthropus*, or Java
man, with a brain size of 800 to 900 c.c., was already capable
of using language and perhaps on the verge of doing so. This
would mean that Peking man, related to Java man but with a
distinctly larger brain, had already become relatively fluent.
Actually, Peking man, as I have already indicated, had a
brain capacity just below minimum group averages of today,
and about 200 to 300 c.c. less than the modal figure for
living populations. This alone would make it very likely that
he possessed speech and communicated by words. What relationship this ancient tongue might have had to any of the
modern families of language, no one can say. If glotto-
chronology, the study of the rate of linguistic change, had
any validity in those days, we should certainly expect that
after 500,000 years its descendant languages would now be
completely different.

Unfortunately, this hypothetical reconstruction of the
timing of the development of language, although it may
eventually prove to have some validity, appears to be somewhat inconsistent with recent studies by Lieberman, Crelin
and Klatt on the ability to produce the sounds that they are
convinced are essential for the development of language.
Taking issue with a widespread assumption that almost any
sounds can be converted into language, they point out that
the ability to clearly enunciate three essential vowels, *a*, *i*,
and *u*, and a number of consonants is basic to the complex

development of modern language. But to produce these sounds, the larynx and its adjacent sound chambers and the tongue's flexibility must have undergone basic modifications. The control of this mechanism, like the control of the pipes of an organ, enables man to produce a wide variety of sounds that can then be assembled into syllables and words.

When these investigators, using a computerized technique and models of the sound chambers, examined an adult modern man, a newborn *sapiens* child, a chimpanzee and the fossil remains of a Neanderthal man from La Chapelle-aux Saints, they found some interesting results. The anatomy of the newborn child and the chimpanzee were clearly inadequate to produce the sounds essential for language, in particular the three basic vowels. Neanderthal man was also found, according to their reconstructed model, to be able with his laryngeal equipment to have produced only a primitive type of language. Given the fact that Neanderthal man had a cranial capacity comparable to our own and that he lived only 40,000 to 50,000 years ago—long after Peking man had become extinct—this conclusion would seem to rule out the probability that Peking man had acquired the capacity and ability to use language.

But, on the other hand, the research on which this conclusion rests, although interesting and possibly definitive, has not yet been subjected to a complete critical evaluation. And, equally important, we know from the archeological record that Neanderthal man had reached a respectable level of technological development, and he has left evidence as well of a fairly high degree of cultural sophistication. This would seem quite incompatible with the low level of linguistic ability that Lieberman, Crelin and Klatt are able to attribute to him.

In any case, if Neanderthal man could use even a primitive language, this would suggest that Peking man also was capable of some degree of linguistic expression, since his anatomical equipment for sound production is not significantly more undeveloped than that of Neanderthal man.

In trying to reconstruct the kind of life the *Sinanthropines* lived, one important aspect would certainly be the size and concentration of the community they formed. This is of special interest in today's world, with its increasing sensitivity to the effect of population density on the quality of life. The actual count of individuals represented by fossil remains has been estimated by Weidenreich to have been about forty, although this figure is approximate since it is based on the judgment of which fragments can be joined to any one individual. As far as cranial and facial bits and pieces are concerned, the problem generally is not too difficult. It becomes increasingly so, however, as it involves linking skeletal bones with crania or assembling stray teeth into one dentition; but estimates of age, sex and robusticity help, and size and the degree of wear can be highly significant in organizing the teeth. Even allowing for some misjudgment, Weidenreich's estimate cannot be very far off.

Unfortunately, we cannot conclude that the community consisted of approximately this number. In the first place, the fossil population cannot be shown to have been strictly contemporaneous. From the geological evidence alone, the actual time span it represents is considerable. And, from the paleontological point of view, not all who die fossilize. Only a tiny percentage of any population survives in a fossilized state.

Our best reconstruction, then, of the size of the prehistoric community can come from parallels we can draw from living populations supporting themselves in a similar hunting–gathering economy. Three interrelated factors become immediately significant. One is the abundance of the natural resources available. The second is how much territory has to be covered to provide an adequate amount of food per person. The amount of seeds and fruits would be limited at certain seasons in temperate areas, particularly in forested regions. This means, of course, that the number of people who can be supported in any one area will also be determined by the distance that the hunter and the gatherer can cover on foot. For the women, expeditions that require extended absence would be unworkable considering their other responsibilities for children and family. Although the men can conceivably make longer journeys in pursuit of game, having to carry the kill home over long distances could also be a major deterrent to wide forays.

The third factor is the technology available for hunting animals. This can make a great difference in what a given region can be made to yield. For example, the arctic coast of Alaska would present an unlikely, indeed a most forbidding ecology for a people with a simple, unsophisticated equipment for hunting even though rich supplies of meat exist there. In fact, the Eskimo have highly specialized technology—harpoons, bladders, boats—with which they can gather abundant stores of meat close to the shores where their villages are conveniently located. When I visited Point Hope, Alaska, in 1941, the village there had a population of four to five hundred. Although they had already been affected in some ways by the introduction of Western ideas and culture, their food supplies were still very largely traditional and were collected by methods virtually unchanged for centuries. This community, which would be regarded as very large for the average hunting–gathering area, was nevertheless abundantly fed. The annual expected kill of whales was between four and eight. And each whale furnished tons of meat—too much to be consumed fresh. The excess was frozen in underground pits. When I arrived in May the natives staged an elaborate ceremony in which we all partook of the somewhat putrescent remains of the preceding year's catch and finished with fresh blubber from the new year's haul. In addition to the whaling, there was a constant gathering in of seals and fish, as well as land animals which were hunted at some distance from the village. Rich and ample as these supplies were, no people without the appropriate specialized gear could have maintained themselves there. It is obvious that a primitive people like the *Sinanthropines*, with their relatively limited technology, would never have made it even with a greatly reduced population.

Specific data on group size in hunting–gathering cultures was assembled some years ago by Julian H. Steward from a wide range of studies covering people in various parts of the world, living under diverse conditions. Among twenty-three such groups studied, the smallest band numbered 20 individuals and the largest 700. The latter, however, was quite exceptional. About half of the groups ranged between 35 and 150, and the rest were equally divided between smaller and larger groups.

The amount of territory required to support one individual varied from about one square mile to an extreme of 86 square miles. The latter figure was derived from a group living in Canada in a subarctic area where conditions were extremely severe. On the whole, three to five square miles per person was about average. Steward concluded that 100 square miles was a fair approximation of what such bands could conveniently manage. Some groups required somewhat more, but 500 square miles seemed to be the normal limit, except in a very few severe cases of ecological poverty.

Since these were all modern groups and presumably equipped with a better technology than Peking man had, it is most unlikely that the band at Chou Kou Tien ever reached the larger numbers found in some of the recent hunting–gathering communities. But since they had the physical endurance to have covered an added area on foot to make up for their primitive equipment, I think it reasonable to conclude that they might have reached the more moderate concentrations found in living bands. Fifty or sixty therefore seems a plausible estimate for the size of the Chou Kou Tien population though, of course, the number would have fluctuated under varying circumstances.

From analyses of the structure of recent groups, it can also be deduced that the Peking population embraced a number of families. This seems to be a universal characteristic of such bands. A number of families living together can provide the mutual cooperation that would inevitably make for a more secure existence. Not only would the men need assistance in hunting and carrying heavy carcasses back to the home cave, but in times of strife with neighboring groups or in defending their essential territory, an adequate number of able-bodied men could mean survival.

The fact that a number of families lived together might well have raised problems of dominance and authority. In many primate groups, this is resolved by a linear arrangement with one male at the top exerting control over the other males in the successive rungs of the ladder. More frequently in modern hunting–gathering groups, it is simply a matter of the best hunter or the stoutest warrior taking the lead in specific situations. I suspect that a similar solution prevailed at Chou Kou Tien.

The sharing of food and game can also be a critical factor. A serious disabling injury to the male head of a single family living in isolation could mean their extinction. But in a joint community such a disaster could be avoided by the mutual assistance of a close-knit group of families.

Not to be minimized as an attraction for group family living is the social and personal satisfaction that it provides. Even today among the experimental young, communes and other group arrangements are generally multifamilial and are based not only on work cooperation but on social needs.

Finally, it would have been essential for the Peking population to have embraced more than a single family since the territory that such a relatively small group could be expected to maintain would scarcely provide an adequate variety of resources. Wild game wander over a considerable area and often food plants scarce in one region may be abundant in another. In other words, a viable hunting–gathering band needs a fair range of territory which only a community of families could hold and protect for its exploitation.

It is not at all uncommon, in fact quite usual, for such hunting–gathering groups to lead a somewhat nomadic existence, moving from one place to another as they exhaust the wild game and plant food. Or they may make expeditions to areas noted for their special seasonal foods. Usually these excursions from the so-called home base are confined to recognized areas. Despite the mobility, the groups cannot expand beyond the limits imposed by the radius of exploitation that foot travel and natural resources impose. Thus a hunting–gathering community can never become large or stable enough to constitute what we would call a town or village.

Although no contemporary and neighboring groups are known, it is most improbable that the Chou Kou Tien community was completely isolated. There must have been a population from which it was derived and to which it was closely related. The normal distribution for any species or race is continuous rather than a series of disconnected, widely scattered and isolated populations. And commonly, there is a distinct cline, or gradual variation, in some physical characteristics as one moves from one extreme of the distribution to another. Thus we would have expected, if we had visited these *Sinanthropines*, to find neighboring groups looking pretty much as they did, but becoming more distinctive as one traveled further away from them.

Having neighbors would have provided the Peking population with occasions for both pleasure and strife. We have only to observe our own behavior and that of our primate relatives to recognize these influences. Inevitably, some conflict would have arisen from the encroachments of a neighboring group on territory regarded by the Chou Kou Tien group as peculiarly theirs. Or the *Sinanthropines* themselves might have run into trouble by doing the same to a nearby band.

Another source of conflict could have been cultural. The propensity of man to judge other peoples by the level of their culture is widespread. The Greeks of 2,500 years ago had contempt for the *barbaroi*, whose languages were incomprehensible to them. The Romans were not much better in their judgments of the Germans and the Britons. When we look at the history of Europe, it is astonishing how persistent the tradition of cultural differentiation has been, and what deep hostility survives even today between ancient neighbors who differ in cultural details. The animosity between the Flamands and Walloons of Belgium permeates many aspects of the national existence. The Basques have a long tradition of enmity with their Spanish neighbors. And the Welsh, Scots and Bretons, despite centuries of integration in their respective nations, still harbor strong feelings of cultural identity and resentment against their English and French compatriots.

The sense of identity with one's own group and the disdain for any other with cultural habits and patterns foreign to one's own are powerful motivating forces not always fully understood. How easily and quickly even today we denigrate a people or a nation because it behaves in patterns that differ from ours. For these reasons then, I suspect there might well have been feelings of suspicion and enmity between the Chou Kou Tien people and some of their neighbors. For although their neighbors probably were closely related racially, cultural differences could have arisen given the relative isolation that populations at that time must have experienced. And, in addition, the local shifting and migration may have brought to their borders relatively distant groups with an even more independent cultural history.

At the same time, feelings of friendship and good will could have existed with other neighboring groups. I am reminded again here of the Marquesan situation. On the island of Nuku Hiva, the entire population was pretty much of the same origin and spoke the same language. Yet the various valleys had developed traditions of deep enmity and constant warfare with some, and friendly interchange with others. We can envision for the Chou Kou Tien population, then, a life that was highlighted and intensified by their relations, hostile and/or pleasurable, with nearby groups.

One of the outstanding features of Peking man's limited

control of his environment was his knowledge and use of fire. All living forms on the surface of the earth where fire can occur naturally are as terrified of it as we are when faced with its ravishing and destructive potential. Even a slight experience with the devastating nature of fire can leave a permanent dread and fear of it.

It is easy then to understand why during the millions of years of man's emergence there is no evidence whatever that he used fire when obviously he must have been aware of its existence. In those early days before the appearance of Peking man, the evolving hominids, as far as we know, were restricted to tropical and perhaps semitropical regions; and fire, except for its warmth, had little or no value. Since cooked food was unknown, this can scarcely be cited as an inducement to experiment with it. It is, of course, possible that animals accidentally caught by fire and roasted may have been sampled by some of the early hominids and aroused a taste that led to the deliberate use of fire; but the problem of the discovery of a technique to make fire and control it remains difficult to resolve.

There may also have been an environmental factor in the recognition of the benign value of fire to organisms living in cold climates. It is of interest that the earliest evidence of its control is found in such areas as Chou Kou Tien, Vèrtesszöllös in Hungary and the Escale cave in France, where the rigors of the climate would have made fire a valuable aid. Sitting or sleeping in a cave near a fire during a cold winter day or night would have made life much more bearable than it might otherwise have been. And this knowledge and use of fire might have been one of the factors that permitted the tropically adapted early hominids to explore and move into a wider range of territory. It is clear that the hominids at this stage had enormously extended their geographic distribution.

When Peking man was first discovered, the traces of fire found in his dwelling sites were identified as the earliest evidence of its planned use by man. Since then, two sites excavated in Europe have suggested that man-made or man-used fire goes back to an even earlier date. Both these sites are placed in the Mindel glaciation, the Escale cave perhaps at the very beginning of this glacial period. If these dates prove to be accurate, it would imply that man's use of fire did not begin in China. If it did begin in Europe, its use may have spread to other regions of the earth. But there still remains the possibility that Peking man discovered the value of fire independently, even if somewhat belatedly. If warmth were the initial use man found for it, cooking would certainly have been quickly discovered as an additional function. Since Peking man knew nothing of pottery and there are no traces of any other kind of receptacle, roasting could have been the only cooking method. And, indeed, this is the technique that most present-day hunting–gathering people employ.

How the fire was made, we don't know. The choices, however, are limited. Aside from using the remnants of natural fires set off by lightning, it could have been started either by striking sparks with appropriate stones or by rubbing sticks together until the heat of the friction ignited the tinder. No other primitive methods are known. Once a fire was kindled, tending it could have become an important function, since this would eliminate the labor of starting another. It would also provide a convenient source for starting fresh hearths in the neighborhood. The fire could then take on something of a precious quality and would require someone to watch over it and keep it alive. One cannot but wonder if the sacred fire in the Greek and other temples, watched and presided over by dedicated maidens, didn't have its origin hundreds of thousands of years before in the precious hearths of Chou Kou Tien, Vèrtesszöllös and Escale.

In any case, this invaluable technology made Peking man's life far more comfortable than it otherwise would have been. In the cold seasons the hearth would have been the center of family life, providing heat to the assembled members and roasted food for their more sophisticated meals. These were, of course, eaten with their hands, since neither chopsticks nor knives and forks appear to have been known—although it is remotely possible that the former might already have been in use in some crude form.

It is worth noting that this control and use of fire represents a kind of landmark in the history of human technology, and of man's adaption to it. Early man had undoubtedly used other sources of natural energy. He might, for example, have ridden a log on a flowing stream. He clearly used the energy latent in the food he gathered and hunted. But until he conquered fire, learned how to make it and control it for his own purposes, he had not gone beyond other animals who use natural energy but lack the ability to manipulate it deliberately. In a sense, one can say that Peking man represents the initial stage of a sequence that was to lead mankind to the discovery of water mills, windmills, sails, steam and gas engines, electricity and atomic power, and the extraordinary complexity of mechanical and technological accessories that make up our modern world. This was the fateful beginning of the use of natural power and energy.

Whether or not the *Sinanthropines* had progressed beyond purely material concerns, with total concentration on getting a living from the environment and satisfying other strictly physiological needs, is hard to say with any solid conviction. There must obviously have been a degree of affection and mutual concern among them. These emotions and needs go deep into man's primate and even his mammalian past. Certainly, maternal solicitude and love would have played a considerable role in their lives, for these attributes are built into the evolution of higher organisms that produce more or less helpless young. Without them, the *Sinanthropines* could not have survived to continue their course and the line would have ceased. And affection between mates would have found expression in this primitive people, as it does in still more primitive creatures. One can even assume that in a people so far from the earliest hominid beginnings, and relatively so near to modern man, love as we know it between conjugal partners might also have existed.

But what is perhaps one of the most distinctive of all human traits, compared with those of other primates or, indeed, other animals, is an intellectual and psychological emotion that emerges from man's wonder and concern about the nature of the world he lives in, his role and his future. Curiosity about these aspects of life and the need to have some explanation for them find expression among almost all living people, at whatever cultural level they may have achieved. The sophistication of one's intellectual environment is no measure of a people's concern with such matters. We find even the simplest cultures having origin myths and various conceptions of the way in which the earth and even the universe are structured and operate. Gods with supernatural powers are conceived as forces that may be propitiated and wooed, and spirits of various kinds and propensities inhabit their visible and invisible world. There is often a sense of mysticism that plays a profound role, not only in the purely religious preoccupations, but also in many details of everyday life. In some cases it may permeate it to such an extent that religion and culture can scarcely be divorced.

This universal recognition and acceptance of a supernatural power or powers does not, of course, mean that the concepts do not show an increasing sophistication from the ideas common in primitive societies to the subtle and highly developed religious systems of modern civilizations. Religion, like other human conceptual systems, has a history of increasing refinement. But my point remains valid that with man we first encounter a level of intellectual development that requires an explanation of the world and its phenomena.

The only way we might know that any prehistoric or pre-*Homo sapiens* populations had reached this point in human development would be through the discovery of shrines, temples or figures representing gods and goddesses and other supernatural powers, or by the survival of some material object that symbolized an aspect of their religious systems. But in a culture as primitive as that of Peking man, we can not conclude from the absence of such highly developed structures as shrines or temples that no such ideas existed. These are technologically far beyond the stage that Peking man had reached. Similarly, even a simple carving of a deity would require tools that he did not possess. It is, of course, conceivable that he treasured natural objects of bizarre shapes, which he might have interpreted as signs of divine powers, and which we would not recognize as part of his archeological heritage. And, equally, he might have kept perishable objects made by his simple devices to serve the same purpose, but whose significance would have been lost to us even had they survived.

One of the few signs that might point to his being already involved with mystical and religious considerations would be evidence of formal burial. If bodies were deliberately interred, with evidence of directional orientation, if such graves contained furnishings for use in the hereafter, if the bodies were arranged in particular ways—such as fully extended or with knees drawn up to the chest, or the corpse on its side—these would certainly imply a standard ritual and a belief in the world after death. And such a sophisticated concept would suggest that it did not exist alone, but was part of a larger, more inclusive mystical and religious system comparable to what we know exists in the simpler cultures of our own time.

Actually, formal burials appear late in human prehistory. Not until we reach Neanderthal man, roughly 400,000 years after Peking man existed, do we find this kind of evidence. None of the fossils from Chou Kou Tien give any indication that they were deliberately interred in any ritualistic fashion. We can, of course, conclude from this and from the absence of any other evidence of religious concepts that the *Sinanthropines* were still unconcerned with the nature, origin and function of the world they lived in and with the meaning of life and its possible immortality. I suspect, however, that we would be doing them some injustice.

5

THE EVOLUTIONARY SETTING

It was almost fifty years ago that Peking man, immediately on his discovery, was recognized as a distinct form of early man—so distinct, in the opinion of Davidson Black, as to warrant his being identified as a representative of a totally separate genus of hominid, *Sinanthropus pekinensis*. Although this judgment was subsequently toned down, he continued for some time, to provide, along with his close relative *Pithecanthropus erectus* from Java, our only conception of what primitive man was like. Today, with the astonishing array of still earlier and still more primitive hominids discovered principally in South and East Africa, the position of Peking man in the sequence of evolutionary stages leading to *Homo sapiens* takes on a very different aspect. This, of course, illustrates that the reconstruction of the evolutionary sequence leading to modern man has itself an evolutionary history. The contemporary gaps in the fossil record, the effect of chance in the sequence of discoveries, the interplay between established hypotheses and new evidence that challenges these entrenched concepts have all played their part in the unfolding drama. The intellectual history of the reconstruction of human evolution has been generally ignored. But in assessing our present views of the place Peking man occupies, it is, I think, of considerable interest and perhaps essential to examine something of the background of the subject and how it has affected these judgments.

For this history has influenced not only our assignment of Peking man as a marker on the trail to *Homo sapiens*, but also our conception of him as the product of a combination of dynamic factors and adaptive processes. Thus, we can examine Peking man's relationship to other known fossils to determine his place in the sequence of evolving hominids. But equally fundamental is an understanding of the significance of the changes that occurred in the course of human evolution, for these, in fact, determine and underlie the sequential and classificatory arrangements.

The reconstruction of the evolution of any species, including man, is a little like fitting together a picture puzzle when the pieces are not all there. Just as one, under these circumstances, might arrange the pieces at hand in a tentative way, using such clues as color patterns, edges and projected design, so the paleontologist, with large empty spaces and with only a small fraction of the forms that define the continuity of an evolutionary line, is forced to use as guides the insights based on comparative anatomy and the theoretical patterns that have been suggested by previous research. And then, to continue the analogy, if you later discover pieces that had been lost under the table, you may either find that they fit nicely into your tentative arrangement or you may have to do a major reshuffling.

When you think how complex an unfinished reconstruction appears, it becomes astonishing in retrospect that anyone would have ventured even to attempt one for human evolution a hundred and twenty-five years ago, when there was so little to go on. All that was available then were two pieces of the total pattern. It was only after Darwin published *The Origin of Species*, in 1859, that these two pieces, figuratively swept under the table, suddenly became significant for a serious study of human evolution by means of the fossil record. As early as the end of the eighteenth century, fossils had stimulated the development of the new science of paleontology, as well as providing geology with critical new tools and insights; but an appraisal of the fossil record of man had not been seriously considered. Although we commonly date to Darwin the recognition of evolution as the key to understanding the proliferation and diversification of life, paleontologists and geologists had in fact been flirting with the idea for decades before. Buffon and Cuvier in the late eighteenth century had developed ideas on the subject. And Lamarck, now discredited for his concept of the dynamics involved, nevertheless had as early as 1809 presented a vision of evolutionary change and development. Sir Charles Lyell, one of the key figures in early nineteenth-century geology, gave much thought to what he called the "transmutation" of species. But most of these emergent ideas were focused on the changes over time that could be observed in fossil shells and animals imbedded in superimposed layers of rock and sediments. Man, as possibly subject to similar influences and with a comparable history of modification, was scarcely mentioned. One notable exception, however, was the "chain" of existence that the famous Scottish judge Lord Monboddo suggested as linking man, monkeys and lower forms of life. Boswell's amusement at the idea reflected the common reaction to it. The widely accepted dogma on the origin of man served in part to discourage his inclusion in this process of change. In Western civilizations, where modern science was developing, he was still commonly believed to owe his origin to an act of divine creation and to have remained unchanged down to the present. But equally important was the absence of any fossil record that might insistently have demanded a reconsideration of such a concept. In the absence of a receptive frame of reference, many a valuable clue could well have been overlooked or discarded as meaningless and worthless. One can't help wondering how much of invaluable significance in our own time gets swept away for the lack of an intellectual milieu that might provide the necessary insights into their meaning.

This tendency to misjudge or ignore fundamental data in the absence of a pattern into which they might be fitted is illustrated by the history of the fossil pieces with which the study of human paleontology began. Gibralter man was the first of these, uncovered in 1848 in the site for which he is named. The form and character of the skull were sufficiently distinctive, compared with modern man, to arouse some curiosity, but this subsided quickly. Considering the fossil's enormous historical significance when it was eventually recognized as the first discovered relic of a pre-*Homo sapiens*, it seems astonishing that it was treated so casually. Then, in 1857, the skull now known as Neanderthal man was unearthed in the German valley of the same name and again its distinctive features, especially its massive protruding brow ridge, unlike any form found in modern man, stimulated some speculation. Dr. H. Schaaffhausen, who prepared the original report on its anatomical characteristics, was aware of its remarkable deviation from any of the known living types of mankind; but he was able to conceive of it only as a relic of some "barbarous" race of man inhabiting Europe just before the Celts and the Germans, or possibly one of the wild races of northwestern Europe described by the Latin writers.

Another widely held view was typified by the interpretation advanced by the internationally known pathologist Rudolf Virchow. He had achieved an enviable reputation for his research, and consequently his word carried much weight. In this case, his word was that the skull was simply a pathological form of modern man. There is a condition known today as acromegaly which we now know to be caused by an excessive production of the growth hormone secreted by the pituitary gland. In addition to other symptoms, this syndrome is characterised by a notable bony thickening in the fingers, toes, lower jaw and brow ridge. It was convincingly documented as an endocrine disturbance by a French doctor, Pierre Marie, as recently as the 1890's, when active research on the endocrine system was just getting under way. Although Virchow did not know of the hormone origin of this pathology, he must have been thoroughly aware of its existence since it occurs not infrequently. I suspect it was this that influenced Virchow's judgment on the Neanderthal find. And in all fairness to his erudition, and in the absence of any knowledge of our fossil precursors, I think his error was not altogether unaccountable.

These two discoveries—which mark the beginning of the fossil accumulation that we now use in retracing human evolution—would have been lost and forgotten had they been uncovered a century earlier, prior to the publication of Darwin's book. For now it was to dawn on man for the first time that, as he had changed and evolved in the past, so he would be destined to change and evolve in the future.

It is a strange accident of chance that both these finds represent a type now known as Neanderthal man, and that this was a form that existed in Europe and elsewhere just before modern man, or *Homo sapiens*, made his appearance in these areas. The much earlier types of hominids, the *Australopithecines* of South and East Africa, were not to be discovered until almost three-quarters of a century later.

Thus, the primitiveness of Neanderthal man was overstressed because for a long time he was our only known ancestral form. Although his differences from modern man were visible and real enough, they were exaggerated in a way that might not have been the case if we had found the earliest types of man first and worked our way up to the Neanderthal type.

In the decades following Darwin's epochal publication, interest in the fossil record of man's evolution became intense, at least in scientific circles, among anatomists, anthropologists, paleontologists, geologists and medical experts. Thomas Henry Huxley, in England, wrote extensively on the subject and displayed an active interest in the fossils of pre-*Homo sapiens*, using them as significant evidence for the validity of human evolution from a primate ancestry. In

Germany, Haeckel had also become an ardent advocate, and in France, where some of the new discoveries were being made, a school of experts began to emerge.

It was not, however, until 1891–92 that a new find presented science with a far more primitive type of hominid than had previously been known. It created a sensation.

Pithecanthropus erectus was found in Java by Dr. Eugène Dubois, a Dutch physician with a strong interest in fossil man. He had enlisted in the Dutch colonial military service in Java in order to be able to explore that region for fossils. It seems strange in retrospect that he should have picked this island as a promising area, for up to then there had been no evidence of early man in the region. Mammalian fossils, however, had been turned up, and these may have suggested to Dubois that it might also be a rich area to explore for traces of man. He may also have been influenced by the current speculation that placed the origin of man in Asia.

In any event, these new discoveries were made in the bank of the Solo (or Bengawan) River in an undisturbed layer that provided ample geological and paleontological proof of great antiquity. The approximate age of the stratum, which gave a time range for the debris found within it, was at that time somewhat debatable, for geological dating techniques were far less accurate then than they are today. Now, radiocarbon measurements of organic material can date a specimen fairly accurately up to 40,000 to 50,000 years ago. For older strata, where suitable rocks are available, the potassium–argon ratio is commonly used. And, in some areas, paleomagnetic techniques have been employed successfully. Where these methods cannot be applied, the dating depends upon the correlation of a newly discovered stratum with others of known date, or on similarities of the faunal associations. These latter techniques, still the only ones available for many early hominid finds, are far from simple to apply as there are many sources of misjudgment that can lead to a wide range of results. The geological sequences in one region may not be precisely duplicated in another, and faunal associations cannot always preclude the possibility that certain animals, having become extinct in one key area, may have survived for a long time in the region where dates based on their contemporaneity are being established. For these reasons, the initial determination of the geological age of Dubois' discovery varied from late Pliocene to mid-Pleistocene—a range of several million years. More recent reassessment of the basic clues has settled, for the present, on a mid-Pleistocene date, approximately 600,000 to 700,000 years ago. This was, of course, still far earlier than any date that could be assigned to the previously known Neanderthal fossils, whose epoch, in Europe at least, just preceded the appearance there of *Homo sapiens*, some 40,000 to 45,000 years ago.

The fossils that were found in Java consisted of the vault of a skull, three teeth, part of a jawbone and the left femur, or thighbone, which was virtually intact. These fragments could not have represented a burial since they were found over an area about 46 feet in length. Their dispersion suggests either that they were washed into their present position by the Solo River, in whose former bed they had lain, or that they were scattered by some marauding animal and covered by deposits from the river after their dispersal.

The skull vault is low and flat, with traces of a heavy projecting brow ridge backed by scarcely any forehead. Estimates of the cranial capacity vary somewhat, but range around 800 c.c. Even though such a brain size is well above even maximum figures for the biggest-brained anthropoid apes, it is still far below what we know of normal variation in *Homo sapiens*. Compared with the Neanderthal man, the Java fossil skull was also strikingly more primitive in its anatomical features.

The thighbone, however, presented quite a different picture. It was relatively long, suggesting a stature of about 5 feet 8 inches. In its conformation, it was clearly a femur completely adapted to upright posture and to an erect gait.

All the morphological changes in the bony structure that reflect the muscular developments that make this posture possible and normal were present and indistinguishable from what we find in recent man. To many contemporary scientists, there seemed to be a discrepancy here: a skull astonishingly primitive, suggesting an ape, yet with a leg bone indistinguishable from our own. This apparent incompatibility or disharmony was used as an argument that the two fossils did not belong together, but represented two distinct and different types, one very primitive and apelike, the other very possibly a modern man who, by some accident, had become associated with the skull. The distance that separated them in the layer where they were found was brought forward in support of this interpretation.

This reaction to the discovery of *Pithecanthropus erectus* illustrates a common enough phenomenon, not only in human paleontology, but in science generally. As one begins to explore a hitherto unknown or dimly perceived area of research, one begins inevitably with only a few facts or surmises. In the absence of an adequate body of proven and established data, one is obliged to set up some working hypothesis. In an active field with many researchers, a number of competing concepts may be formulated. As new facts and observations are brought to light, they may support one or another of these working hypotheses or they may undermine their validity and force a reexamination of them with a resulting modification to fit the new discoveries.

In an experimental field, the search for new facts can be actively pursued according to the facilities available and the number of workers who are committed to it. Progress, of course, will depend on a number of factors, among them the availability of techniques to arrive at some essential insights.

In human paleontology we find certain problems that have given its progress a somewhat idiosyncratic character as compared with the experimental sciences. The scientist in this field depends primarily on concrete fossil remains, which cannot be created in a laboratory. In the study of the sequence of human stages in the past, it is only the once-living forms, now fossilized and marking the course of the transformation, that offer the evidence we seek. Therefore, paleontologists must find what they need in the geological strata of the past. For a generation before the discovery of *Pithecanthropus,* students of human evolution had been deeply influenced in their conceptions of early man by their studies of the living anthropoid apes. Although opinions varied as to which of these was the most likely candidate for relationship with man's hominid ancestor, it was widely believed that the transition from an apelike precursor to a primitive hominid would be marked by a series of symmetrical and harmonious changes that had gradually and concurrently affected the various parts of the anatomy. Thus, an enlargement of the brain toward hominid levels would be closely correlated with a harmonious or symmetrical development of upright posture. That a marked development toward erect posture might have occurred independently of any change in brain size—and indeed might have been one of the triggering factors for a later enlargement of the brain —was not inferred from any of the available evidence. In the absence of any recognized fossil data covering the earliest stages of hominid evolution, this unchallenged conception was ultimately destined to influence the first reaction to fossils that did represent these earlier phases of human evolution.

This raises the question of why the fossil evidence was, and to a considerable extent still is, slow in coming to light. There is an interesting background here that reflects the importance of social, cultural and intellectual factors in affecting the progress of a scientific field such as this. First of all, how do you find human fossils? Where do you look? And even if you suspect an area will yield some evidence, where exactly would you dig, or spot the tiny fragments you seek?

In the early days, most if not all fossils were accidental discoveries. Excavating gravel pits, building roads, ploughing and various other disturbances of the earth's surface for

man's technological needs would, on very rare occasions, dis-
close stone artifacts and, more infrequently, skeletal remains. Until archaeology provided man with an insight into
the meaning of the cultural relics of the past, they were
ignored and discarded. By the early nineteenth century,
such accidental finds began to attract the attention of the
excavators, who had become aware of their possible value
and the interest that archaeologists displayed in them. Thus,
more and more, these chance finds were likely to be brought
to the attention of experts who could assess their significance. In a very small proportion of such discoveries human
fossils have been found, but, as we have noted, it was not
until after Darwin that these rare markers of human evolution got the attention they deserved.

The reason why most of these fossils were first found in
Europe was not because they were more abundant there, but
rather was the result of a more advanced technology and a
wider awareness of their significance. In the latter half of
the nineteenth century the natives of Asia and Africa had
little if any knowledge of the meaning and worth of these
relics and would have been most unlikely to bring them to
anyone's attention, if indeed there were anyone around who
might have known what to do with them.

In addition to such finds by chance, archaeologists had
developed explorative techniques of their own for cultural
remains, and many of the Neanderthal and early *Homo sapiens* fossils came to our attention through such archaeological
activity. Another important source of new hominid discoveries has been the search by paleontologists for animal fossils. Peking man himself was discovered in this way. I have
already described the circumstances that led Dr. Andersson
and his paleontological colleagues in China to the site where
they found this early man.

Thus, until Dubois deliberately went to Java with the
purpose of searching for fossils, human paleontologists
knew only a limited range of European material. New evidence was slow in reaching appropriate laboratories, and

most of it represented only a small and late segment of the story. It was not, until another generation had passed that special expeditions to search for these traces of early man began to be organized. Some of them, like Roy Chapman Andrews' Mongolian expeditions in the 1920's, which I have already mentioned, found animal fossils considerably more abundant than human ones.

In the last thirty or forty years, these planned explorations have become increasingly more numerous, and in some cases they have yielded results that have added immeasurably to our knowledge of the subject. Dr. Robert Broom, a physician turned paleontologist, was one of the first in South Africa to pursue these searches. Ralph von Koenigswald's assemblage of fossils gathered in Java in the late 1930's represents still another organized search that paid off. Since then, Louis Leakey, Howell and others have explored promising areas in East Africa, which also fortunately lived up to expectations. Despite all these developments, chance discoveries will continue to be made as they have been in the past.

Any doubts that might have lingered about the association of the traits assigned to *Pithecanthropus* were effectively extinguished some forty years after his discovery by a series of new finds made in Java by Von Koenigswald. Some of them came from somewhat earlier and older levels, and others were coeval with Dubois' find. There were jaws, parts of the face and other skeletal fragments that confirmed unquestionably that *Pithecanthropus* was a fully erect hominid with a skull that nonetheless revealed traces of his apelike origins.

Among the specimens Von Koenigswald discovered was a type more primitive than *Pithecanthropus* and possibly ancestral to him. He was named *Meganthropus*. This hominid holds a special interest since it has been dated back to about a million years ago and apparently has a counterpart found in South Africa.

Just before *Sinanthropus* was first identified in the fossil debris of Chou Kou Tien, another chance discovery was made in South Africa in 1924. This was the skull of *Australopithecus africanus*. Some eighty miles from Witwatersrand, the blasting of a limestone bed had turned up a fossilized primate skull that was brought to the attention of Raymond Dart, a professor of anatomy at the University of Witwatersrand. With a geological colleague, he decided to explore the site. Among some more of these specimens that they found was one that especially drew Dart's interest. This fossil was damaged, part of the vault and face having been broken off and lost, but sufficiently complete to give a very adequate representation of what the whole skull had been like. It was an immature individual, about five or six years old, judging from the teeth present. Allowing for the changes that come with age, the mature form was judged then to be very primitive and apelike. In the adult form its brain size would have been only a little above that of the anthropoid apes.

When Raymond Dart announced his find and published a description of it in 1925, he was influenced in his judgment by the established concepts then current. Despite its overall apelike character, he was obviously impressed by some suggestions of a development in a hominid direction, and he noted in particular its anatomical adjustments to a more upright posture than is characteristic for any ape. Yet he did not at first venture to identify it as the earliest representative of the emergent human line that had as yet come to light. In fact, the name he gave it is highly indicative of his first assessment. He called this young specimen *Australopithecus africanus*—the southern ape from Africa.

The general professional reaction was skeptical of any suggestion that here was a new marker for the course that human evolution had followed. Sir Arthur Keith, one of the leading contemporary authorities, rejected *Australopithecus* as belonging in the sequence leading to man. As late as 1931, when Professor Earnest Hooton in the United States published *Up From the Ape*, one of the standard books on the subject, he didn't even mention the fossil as having any significance for human evolution. As a devoted student of Hooton's, I hasten to add that this failure was not a reflection on his competence but the consequence of the normal conservatism in scientific research which, as I have already pointed out, was somewhat intensified in this area of the reconstruction of human evolution. The human paleontologists, who were busy with the new discoveries in China failed to see any relevance of this find to their own fossils.

The initial rejection of *Australopithecus* as being close to or actually in the line leading to man is not unexpected. This skepticism has occurred over and over again in many branches of science. And one can make out a good case that this should be so. If every new discovery in any field of science were to be uncritically accepted, it would play havoc with the firm growth of the structure. Hard-boiled skepticism that requires overwhelming proof may be frustrating to an innovator, and it can often slow things down, but in the long run it can also be an insurance against ill-advised and hasty conclusions.

In part, I suspect, the revolution in our evaluation of this ancient child was strongly reinforced by the subsequent discovery of an ever-increasing series of both closely related and somewhat deviant types. These have been found in a number of sites in South and East Africa, and their time span covers perhaps as much as 3 to 4 million years. The procession begun by *Australopithecus* in 1924 was joined by fossils uncovered by Dr. Robert Broom in 1934. Broom was a Scottish physician settled in South Africa. When I first met him, while he was visiting New York in the 1930's, he presented a fascinating combination of a rather old-fashioned, slightly shabby gentleman in a wing collar, and an almost fanatical devotee absorbed in his paleontological interests. He talked shop and little else.

As these new discoveries were being made by Broom, Dart, Robinson and others, and then announced to the scientific world and to the world press, they were ushered onto the stage with great èclat and were given names that emphasized their uniqueness. In addition to the first in the parade, *Australopithecus africanus*, the cast for "Early Man" soon included *Paranthropus robustus*, *Paranthropus crassidens*, *Plesianthropus transvaalensis*, *Australopithecus prometheus* and *Telanthropus capensis*.

To these, two more were added in the 1960's as a result of the remarkable persistence of a thoroughly dedicated fossil hunter—Dr. Louis S. B. Leakey. The son of an English physician settled in Kenya, Leakey had from his childhood been exposed to the indigenous culture and had developed a deep interest in it. In retrospect, it seems completely natural that, as a result, he would have pursued anthropological studies during his days at Cambridge. On returning to Kenya after his English education, he began a professional career as an archeologist. These deliberate probings into the past opened up to him the related problems of early man and his fossil history, to which the latter part of Leakey's career was devoted almost completely. The site to which he chose to devote most of his attention was the Olduvai Gorge in Tanganyika, where successive geological strata are exposed. Geologically, this means that for hundreds of miles ancient strata are open to inspection that could otherwise have been uncovered only at unbelievable expense and superhuman effort. By examining them for fossils accidentally exposed by the erosion of the steep banks or washed down to their base, he could, if patient and acute enough, hope to find clues for further exploration and even excavation. After some years of fieldwork, which had become a dynastic family affair involving his wife, Mary, and his sons, Leakey was rewarded with the now-famous discovery of "Zinj" in 1959. *Zinjanthropus boisei* was found by Mrs. Leakey in its original location in a layer that was subsequently dated by the potassium–argon technique at about 1,750,000 years ago. In his first announcements of the discovery, Leakey stressed the distinctive character of this new hominid, not only by giving it a separate generic classification, but by emphasizing its points of difference with the other early African hominid fossils. Zinj had a particularly massive cranial structure and even a ridge of bone running front to back along the top mid-line of the skull—the result, clearly, of the extensive development of the temporal muscles, which aid the chewing function of the jaw. When these muscles become so highly developed that they cover the top of the skull where the right and left segments meet, they tend to produce a ridge of bone for additional attachment We see this frequently in the gorilla, who is endowed with similar massive muscles. In the dentition and other features as well, Zinj presented equally distinctive features that encouraged Leakey to hail him as a new type.

In the following year still another find was made in the same neighborhood, but in a slightly lower horizon and with a date close to 2 million years ago. Curiously enough, this one—*Homo habilis*—although somewhat older, was far less primitive and had a somewhat larger brain. Again, as is typical on the first appearance of so many fossils, it was billed as a new star with special rating.

Subsequent finds at Lake Rudolph, Omo and other sites in East Africa have now extended the time span of this stage of hominid evolution back as far as 4 to 5 million years ago, into the Pliocene, and up to as recent as 600,000 years ago.

When the *Australopithecines* first began to emerge, there was a tendency to give each new find as distinctive a classification as possible. Partly, this was the result of a natural human tendency to enhance the importance of one's own discovery. To find simply another representative of a well-known fossil type has its value, certainly for the expert interested in the range of variation that the type might display. But how much more acclaim can be expected when one discovers a hitherto-unknown species or genus.

The scientific difficulty of establishing legitimate resemblances and differences has also encouraged the proliferation of types. No human population any more than any animal or plant population is absolutely uniform, variation being a universal characteristic of organic life. But if you have only one representative of such a population it can be difficult to establish its normal range of variation, which might then serve as a measure by which to include or exclude other fossil candidates. When *Australopithecus africanus* was first reported by Dart in 1925, he and others had to infer what the adult of this new type of early man was like from an immature and incomplete specimen. Under the circumstances, it would not be easy to set up the normal range one might expect among other members of this group. In the absence of such a guide, a second find of the same population, if deviant enough, could be misinterpreted as belonging to an altogether distinct type. This too undoubtedly contributed to the creation of a plethora of supposedly distinctive and disparate types that were presumed to have flourished at this stage of human evolution.

Sex differences are also sometimes misread as type or species distinctions when a sample is too impoverished or scanty to provide evidence for establishing such basic anatomical differentiation.

As more of these *Australopithecines* and related forms accumulated, it became increasingly obvious that the proliferation of variant types at this stage of human evolution had been grossly exaggerated. It now became possible to reassess these fossils in terms of sex difference and normal type variations. As a result, many students are inclined to recognize only two types of *Australopithecines*: one subtitled *africanus* and the other, *robustus*. The former represents a relatively less rugged variant and the latter a heavier, more muscular type with some specializations of its own.

The dental differences between these two manlike primates have been attributed by Clifford Jolly, Professor of Anthropology at New York University, and by others to the fact that *Australopithecus robustus* became adapted to a seed diet which required the distinctly large molars that he developed. *Australopithecus africanus*, on the contrary, taking to small game as well as to the traditional fruit diet of his primate ancestors, became virtually omnivorous with different dental requirements that are more in keeping with a form ancestral to modern man.

But even as I write, new discoveries are being reported at various points along the Rift Valley of East Africa that may make new assessments and conclusions necessary. Already four or five organized research teams have been established to recover early hominid relics and to collect evidence for the reconstruction of the ecology in which these early hominids lived. These are the most sophisticated efforts to find fossils in the history of human paleontology and illustrate a development I have already mentioned. In fact, they remind one a little of a kind of gold rush, with a staking out of claims and with more than a touch of competition.

These organized searches have proven extraordinarily productive. At Lake Rudolph alone, if we count the scattered teeth, hundreds of finds are made during each field season. Since the analysis of this wealth of material may well take years to complete, the present conclusions I have mentioned can only be regarded as tentative. Before passing on to other phases of this history, however, I should mention that there is some reason to believe that, even as early as two million years ago, still another type of hominid, showing a notably larger brain size, may have appeared in East Africa and lived contemporaneously with the two types of *Australopithecines* now generally recognized. *Homo habilis*, discovered by Leakey senior, appears to be confirmed by finds made by Leakey junior.

No sooner had the *Australopithecines* become firmly established as the earliest known hominids ancestral to modern man, than an announcement in 1961 by Professor Elwyn L. Simons of Yale University seriously undermined this distinction. His candidate for the role was *Ramapithecus brevirostris*, a fossil found in the Siwalik hills of India about thirty years before. Here was a case, not of a new discovery, but of mistaken identity. The story of this resuscitation goes back to 1910, when Guy Pilgrim, an Englishman searching for fossils in the Siwaliks, discovered what were apparently apelike bones similar to an extinct genus known as *Dryopithecus*, which was already well documented from finds made in Europe. Twenty-one years later, G. Edward Lewis, a Yale graduate student, set off to revisit the sites, which had been neglected since Pilgrim's pioneering exploration. He was well rewarded with a series of new discoveries which he published in 1934. Following Pilgrim's example, he used the names of Hindu gods, heroes and legendary figures for the nomenclature of the new genera he identified. One specimen was called *Brahmapithecus* and another *Ramapithecus*. Lewis, describing the latter, was clearly impressed by its "progressive" traits, fragmentary as the fossil was, and emphasized the possibility that it might represent a hominid-like ape or even an emergent hominid. But this interpretation was rejected by contemporary authorities, and Lewis himself did not press it. As a result, *Ramapithecus* was relegated in the literature to the category of an ape very possibly linked with the well-known *Dryopithecines*. And for years that is where he remained, receiving little or no attention from those eagerly following the trail to man's origins.

Simons, on restudying the Siwalik fossils many years later, was struck by the primitive hominid traits of *Ramapithecus*. Joined by his colleague David Pilbeam, he undertook a detailed examination of the existing *Dryopithecines* and their presumed Siwalik relatives. They came to the conclusion that *Brahmapithecus* and *Ramapithecus* belonged in the same group, and that they represented an early stage of hominid differentiation.

While the *Australopithecines* were now, as a result of new discoveries, being placed back 4 to 5 million years ago, the reestablished hominid *Ramapithecus* was dated to the Miocene-Pliocene, somewhere between 10 and 14 million years before our time. This, of course, gives quite a different aspect to the timing of human evolution, and would have seemed inconceivable a hundred years ago, when the search for man's origins began.

In evaluating the status of *Ramapithecus*, Simons and

Pilbeam had to depend largely on dental characteristics, since the original specimen consisted of a fragment of the upper jaw with some of the teeth and a few empty sockets. Although this may seem scanty evidence for so weighty a decision, the enormous significance of the dentition in establishing relationships and groupings among fossils cannot be overemphasized. The teeth are important here for two reasons. One is that they are just about the most abundant of all fossils. Very often when there are no other skeletal traces, teeth will be found. And many categories, not only among primates, but in other mammals and vertebrates generally, are based on dental evidence alone. The advantage of teeth is that they show distinctive and consistent patterns that are highly characteristic. Shape, size, root structure, cusps, presence or absence of various kinds of teeth, groovings, and enamel structure, are among some of the dental traits that combine to form a wide variety of specialized combinations. An expert has no difficulty in identifying a genus or even a species by its dental characteristics. When one examines the dentition of primates, it becomes evident that as a zoological order they display a line of development of their own, unlike any other, although there are some similarities between the early primates and other primitive mammals. But as the primates evolved, they also developed dental differentiations characteristic of each subdivision. In the hominid line, for example, the projecting canine tooth, so prominent in all the anthropoid apes and monkeys too, has become reduced in size until it rises scarcely, if at all, above the level of the other teeth. This reduction has eliminated in man the need for the space, or slot, called the diastema, into which the projecting canines can fit when the teeth are in occlusion. In man, the incisors are vertical rather than sloping forward. The molars, which in apes are longer than they are wide, have now become wider than they are long. Also, as I have already mentioned, there is a tendency, fully developed in the later forms of man, for the molars to decrease in size from the first to the third, just the reverse from the order in the apes and some other primates. Moreover, the cusp pattern and the number and fusion of the roots of the molars and premolars have distinctive forms in man that differentiate his teeth from those of other primates.

The dentition of *Ramapithecus*, as much as there is of it, shows features one might expect to find in an emergent hominid. The canine is reduced and the form of the molars is more hominid than apelike. Moreover, the shape of the dental arcade, instead of having more or less parallel sides as in the apes, is parabolic and thus resembles the curvature found in hominids. Judging from the size of the jaws, *Ramapithecus* was relatively small and had a reduced snout. At one point, Simons seemed inclined to infer that *Ramapithecus* was upright in his gait. This last deduction, very possibly true, still needs more concrete supportive evidence.

In the course of these investigations it was demonstrated that the separation of *Ramapithecus* and *Brahmapithecus* into separate categories was not justified. Rather, they belonged together, the lower jaw representing *Brahmapithecus* fitting nicely into the upper jaw of *Ramapithecus*.

This dramatic restoration of *Ramapithecus* inevitably led Simons and Pilbeam to reassess other fossils that might, in this new light, reveal relationships that had been obscured. One of their conclusions now favorably received is that *Ramapithecus*, or a closely related type, had also lived in Africa during roughly the same era. The African version was *Kenyapithecus*, which Leakey had discovered. This, of course, suggests a wide distribution of this early hominid, and it still leaves open the question that has been debated since Darwin's time: Where did the human line originate—Asia or Africa?

If *Ramapithecus* and the *Australopithecines* represent the initial stages of the human realm, what can be identified as the Middle Kingdom? At present, this intermediary phase is known as *Homo erectus*, a somewhat misplaced label. Such a group name suggests that upright posture had been slow in developing and was only achieved at this relatively late stage in hominid evolution. Actually, the earlier *Australopithecines* were already adapted to erect posture, and *Homo erectus* had undoubtedly inherited his human gait from these ancestral forms. It is, of course, evident from his skeletal remains that *Homo erectus* had made considerable advances on this adaptation, reaching a level not too different from that characteristic of modern man.

The category of *Homo erectus*, which roughly dates from about 1 million to about 150,000 or 200,000 years ago, includes a number of fossils from various parts of the Old World—Africa, Asia and Europe. Among the better-known are the Heidelberg mandible, the *Pithecanthropus* series and the Ternifine and the Lantian skulls. This is the group into which *Sinanthropus* has been placed. One of the striking features of *Homo erectus* is the very marked increase in the size of the brain. Although this stage of human evolution occupied only a fraction of the time span allotted to *Australopithecus*, the cranial capacity of *Homo erectus* almost doubled. *Pithecanthropus*, another of this group, dated at about 600,000 to 700,000 years ago, had a cranial capacity of about 790 c.c. *Sinanthropus*, who followed him about 100,000 years later, had already reached an average of 1100 c.c., a figure just approaching the minimum average for a small-brained modern *Homo sapiens*. It is dangerous to correlate too closely intelligence with brain size, especially in dealing with normal variation within a group. Although Anatole France is said to have had a cranial capacity of only a little over 1100 c.c. and Von Hindenburg, more than 1800 c.c., it would certainly not be the general judgment that Anatole France was the less intelligent. Yet in the evolutionary history of the hominids this character does show a steady progressive increase and, taken with the evidence of a parallel development of capacity as measured by human technology, language, and other traits, we can only deduce that in a general way the growth of the brain in hominid evolution is indicative of an increasing intelligence. Since the stone tech-

nology that *Homo erectus* left behind him was not yet notable for its highly developed array of mechanical refinements
and specialized techniques such as we see in the range of
tools used by the men of the Upper Paleolithic, the acquisition of language at this stage of human evolution offers the
most likely explanation for the sudden spurt in the already-
increasing brain size characteristic of the earlier hominids.

As we look at *Sinanthropus* in the light of his antecedents now known to us, he takes on quite a different aspect
than he presented to the scientific world when he was first
announced. Then, with only *Pithecanthropus* preceding him
in time, Peking man appeared to the scientists of the day as
a distinctly primitive type of man—just as, some sixty years
before, Neanderthal man had seemed almost apelike to Darwin's contemporaries. But now, with *Australopithecus* and
possibly even *Ramapithecus* as yardsticks, *Sinanthropus* can
be reassessed as well along in the evolutionary transformation. He had achieved a stage only just short of *Homo sapiens*. He walked upright, had a fairly well developed technology, knew and used fire and lived in a hunting–gathering
society not so different as to be altogether unfamiliar to
modern man at the same level of economy. He very probably
spoke a language and could communicate much as we do,
and his brain size was only a little below the minimal level
for *Homo sapiens*.

Following *Homo erectus*, and Peking man, there are
several claimants for the transitional stage before reaching
what may definitely be recognized as *Homo sapiens*. One is
the well-known Neanderthal man, sometimes distinguished
as "classic" Neanderthal, and another is the "progressive"
Neanderthal type that paradoxically, in the European
framework, antedates the "classic" form. A third is Swanscombe man. This is a somewhat complicated situation that I
shall try to clarify by reviewing the historical background. It
has led to a variety of opinions, often advanced with some
heat.

As I have previously mentioned, the Neanderthal man

was the first fossil pre–*Homo sapiens* type to be recognized. By the 1860's, the finds of Gibraltar and Neanderthal man had established that man, like other organisms, had left a record of his evolution. Since these two fragments were all that were known and represented a clearly more primitive type than *Homo sapiens*, in the absence of a wider range of human precursors, their differences were overly emphasized —partly, I suspect, as a natural consequence of the limited material, but also because these fossils were trump cards and could be used more effectively if their apelike qualities were stressed. The heavy brow ridge, the chinless jaw and the low, sloping forehead certainly suggested an apelike form when they were held up against modern man. But compared with actual apes, Neanderthal man appeared very close indeed to *Homo sapiens*. The skull had expanded up to and even beyond modern standards; the face had lost its snout· like character, the nose, though not beaklike, was as prominent as it is in some varieties of man today. As more fossils accumulated, increasing the time span of human evolution, there was considerable controversy in the early twentieth century as to whether or not the "classic" Neanderthal man could have been ancestral to *Homo sapiens*. To many experts, the "primitive" and apelike characteristics of Neanderthal man, although clearly suggestive of a stage through which the hominid succession had passed, nevertheless seemed to argue that he could not have been our immediate antecedent. In fact, some even advanced the idea that he represented a specialized form of man that ended as an extinct offshoot from the main line.

One of the difficulties that plagued those who argued for a Neanderthal ancestry for *Homo sapiens* arose from the more reliable dating techniques that placed *Homo sapiens* right on the heels of Neanderthal man (in the European archaeological sequence) with no sign of any transitional stages. Neanderthal man is closely associated with a well-defined culture known as Mousterian, named for one of the classic sites. It flourished up to about 40,000 years ago, and immediately replacing it came the Upper Paleolithic, with a distinctively different and much more advanced technology and with evidence of artistic expression of a high order. The fabricator of this Upper Paleolithic culture was *Homo sapiens*. Since evolutionary change is relatively slow, there does not seem to have been enough time to allow for the transformation from a Neanderthal to a *sapiens* type. The technological differences between the two cultures were, however, never stressed in these arguments since these attributes of man are less reliable for tracing evolutionary sequence.

This lack of agreement on the precise relationship of Neanderthal man to *Homo sapiens* was complicated still further in the early part of the present century. Swanscombe man was uncovered in England in 1935 and the Steinheim skull in Germany soon after. Although the dating has fluctuated, both are definitely earlier in the European sequence than Neanderthal man, going back 200,000 to 300,000 years. Yet in their general cranial conformation, both are much closer to *Homo sapiens* than is "classic" Neanderthal. Unfortunately, the skulls are not complete, but they do clearly display some of the differences to be expected in a transitional form.

At about the same time, another cluster of finds represented by the Ehringsdorf skull, presented the scientific world with still another type. This one dated to the last interglacial period—about 150,000 years ago—and displayed some Neanderthaloid characteristics (the heavy brow ridge for example), but it also approached modern man much more closely than did the more recent so-called classic Neanderthal. This earlier but more advanced Neanderthaloid type was therefore frequently referred to as a "progressive" Neanderthal.

Finally, one further complexity emerged. In the archeological excavation of a group of caves in Palestine, an English team headed by Miss Dorothy Garrod came upon two series of skulls. One lot was found at a cave known as Skhul, the other in a nearby cave called El Tabun. The responsibility for assembling and studying this material was turned over to Sir Arthur Keith, then the leading British expert on fossil man, who was assisted by a young American student of his, Theodore D. McCown. The first report identified the population as essentially Neanderthal with, however, a number of individuals showing interesting intergrades between this type and modern man. Keith offered two solutions: one, that the fossils represented a region and time (the only one on record) that permitted contact between the two types and therefore some degree of miscegenation; the other, that here was a segment of the Neanderthal population caught in the process of evolutionary change. Subsequently, it became clear that the two caves were not contemporary and that the populations were therefore separated in time. El Tabun turned out to be 10,000 years earlier, and its inhabitants were all Neanderthal. Skhul contained the remains of the more recent and more *sapiens*-like fossils. It still remains, however, a question whether the Skhul series represents a natural evolutionary change or was the result of mixture between an earlier Neanderthal population and an invading *Homo sapiens* strain.

Nowadays there is a growing tendency to minimize the differences between classic Neanderthal man and modern man and to derive the latter directly from the former. The Palestinian cave materials seem to support this idea. But when one examines a classic Neanderthal skull, of which there are now a large number, one cannot escape the conviction that its fundamental anatomical formation is an enlarged and developed version of the *Homo erectus* skull. As in *Homo erectus*, it has the bun-shaped protrusion in the occiput, the heavy brow ridge, the relatively flattened crown that from the rear presents a profile like a gambrel roof. Its greatest breadth is low, just above the ears, and the absence of a jutting chin is typical. When Neanderthal and *Homo sapiens* skulls are placed side by side, the contrast is immediately apparent and unmistakeable. Modern man has a morphological pattern in which the brow ridge is vestigial (showing traces usually only in males), the forehead full and high, the vault distinctly elevated with the skull reaching its greatest width at a level well above the ears, and a chin emerging at last. These are some of the more visible distinctions that differentiate modern man from his Neanderthal predecessor. For this reason I find it difficult to accept an evolutionary transformation within the brief time span that separated the Neanderthal and *sapiens* populations in the European chronology, yet I strongly suspect that the Neanderthal type may well represent a survival of a stage antecedent to modern man.

At this point in our reconstruction of human evolution, we are faced with a variety of pieces of the puzzle with no clear clues for a tidy arrangement. My own interpretation, admittedly speculative—as are the other assorted solutions —may be summarized as follows. Two factors often overlooked in attempts to establish the relationship and connections between fossil types are the inherent tendency of all organisms, including man, to form distinct variants, and for these in the course of the millenia, even the hundreds of thousands of years of their existence, to move in various migratory patterns. The existence today of a wide range of human types is a reflection of this variability. Even a relatively homogenous population that becomes divided into isolated communities will, with sufficient time, develop genetic differences. This has been demonstrated by L. L. Cavalli-Sforza in a recent study of such a series of isolated communities in an Italian valley, and other investigations have shown the same phenomenon. When we contemplate the enormous geographical range of contemporary mankind and the fact that for thousands of years many human populations have been effectively isolated from one another, not even knowing of each other's existence, it becomes understandable that such differences should arise. Thus we have the Australian aborigine, with his relatively primitive anatomical traits, in marked contrast to the mongoloid Chinese or the European.

Similarly, it would be contrary to all biological expectations to imagine that mankind in past stages of evolution was uniform throughout its geographical distribution. Then as now, a variety of types must have existed, some showing a more marked progressive or adaptive change than others that for one reason or another had remained relatively conservative. Thus, while evolutionary changes leading to *Homo sapiens* were developing at a more rapid rate in some populations, others were preserving the older *Homo erectus* pattern with, of course, some modifications. Neanderthal man might well have been one of these. We find a similar conservatism in the contemporary and related fossils of Solo man, found in Java, and Rhodesian man in Africa.

Indeed, the actual fossil record provides us with evidence that the change toward the *sapiens* type was already well under way as early as Swanscombe man, some 200,000 years ago, and very probably also in the Steinheim man, both of which antedate Neanderthal man by at least a couple of hundred thousand years. Another bit of evidence that supports the conception of an earlier transition to *Homo sapiens* than at the classic Neanderthal stage is the Fontechevade skull found in France and dating to the last interglacial, some 100,000 to 150,000 years ago. Finally, the progressive Neanderthal, represented by the Ehringsdorf and other fossils, also predates the European classic Neanderthal population.

The issue then becomes the peculiar sequence—with Neanderthal occupying Europe immediately before *Homo sapiens* made his appearance and then virtually disappearing off the face of the earth. Of course, we cannot answer all the questions this raises. But one solution has occurred to me that goes a long way in providing a reasonable explanation. This involves several dynamic factors of human cultural adaptation, shifting climatic zones and mass migration. First, the classic Neanderthal man's occupation of Europe seems from present data to have been more or less confined to the Würmian glacial period, when Europe below the glacial edge was cold and tundralike, resembling parts of Siberia today. It had a distinctive fauna that no doubt provided food for its human inhabitants. In a sense it could be considered as a kind of refuge area, though one that could be exploited only by a people thoroughly adapted to its rigors and difficulties. Just as no population with a simple culture could manage to live today in the subarctic region without special technological and cultural adaptations, so Europe then must have been equally inhospitable to any population not accustomed to its requirements and skilled in exploiting them. Neanderthal man obviously was, since he lived there.

Homo sapiens comes in and replaces classic Neanderthal man during an interglacial episode when climatic conditions had ameliorated and the environment had become more hospitable and inviting to a people accustomed to living in a more temperate zone. The replacement might have been accomplished by force, or it might simply have been a matter of absorbing the Neanderthal population by miscegenation, an explanation that Carlton Coon has favored. or, in part, the vast majority of the Neanderthal population may simply have retreated, following their receding environment as it moved north and east. We know, for example, that cultural traces of the Mousterian technology, with which Neanderthal men are associated, have been found at much more recent dates in Asiatic Russia, where tundralike subarctic conditions prevailed after they had disappeared in western Europe. We have many examples in human history of whole populations moving with their environments as these shifted with climatic change. Nor is this linkage confined to human groups. It is well known among animals as well.

This migratory pulsation may also explain the appearance in Europe of Swanscombe man in the second interglacial period and of Ehringsdorf and other progressive Neanderthals in the third interglacial. They, too, may have entered Europe during the warm phases of the Pleistocene and retreated as the glacial epochs returned to alter the entire ecology of the continent.

Finally, in the light of available evidence and the probabilities it suggests, I am inclined to believe that the actual transition to *Homo sapiens* may have taken place outside Europe altogether. If our hunting–gathering Paleolithic ancestors were as well adapted to their environments as their descendants, we might expect that they also followed the shifts of climate and the migration of the associated fauna and flora, upon which they were dependent. Learning to use other foods than those to which we are accustomed has always been a genuine difficulty. Even today, the famine-stricken rice-eaters in India reject wheat or accept it with great reluctance. It has also become increasingly clear from the geological evidence that, as the glacial periods recurrently invaded Europe as well as other parts of the Northern hemisphere, the distinct climatic zones moved southward. Thus, the temperate band that now characterizes Europe, as it did in previous interglacial periods, would have been displaced with the onset of glaciation and ended up in northern Africa or even the Sahara, now zones of increasing aridity with vast stretches of desolate and inhospitable desert country. At the peaks of glaciation, these regions, far more temperate and hospitable for human occupation, might well have provided a suitable environment for the evolving *Homo sapiens*. And, in the course of the many thousands of years before the zones moved northward again, there would have been time enough for the final transformation to modern man. With *Homo sapiens* at the end of the last glaciation moving back to Europe with the shifting climatic zones, he would have left the evidence behind him, and we must therefore look elsewhere than in Europe for this final alteration.

In the history of the discovery of the fossil record of man it is significant that at least one insight, the one with which it all began, has survived undiminished. This is the conviction that the human line evolved from some primate ancestor. Nothing has come to light that shakes this deduction in the slightest. And, although it is rarely mentioned in the literature of human paleontology, this basic principle was derived, not from any fossil material whatever, but from the evidence provided by comparative anatomy and systematic zoology. It was Linné, or Linnaeus, the Swedish botanist and systematist, who first linked man with the primates. In his monumental treatise *Systema Naturae*, published in 1732, he assembled the vast literature on the variation of plant and animal life and organized it into a systematic classification based on structural similarities.

Virtually all peoples employ some system for identifying the variations of plant and animal life. In some cases, the recognition of types and groups is extremely sophisticated. The Polynesians not only have special names for the various species of fish that inhabit the waters surrounding the islands, but also a nomenclature that differentiates the successive stages in the life cycle of these creatures. Partly, this is because certain fishes that are a desirable catch at one stage are poisonous or undesirable at another. In addition, because the dependence of many of these islanders on marine life is essential, they have a natural interest in every variation it presents.

But these nomenclatorial devices, so important for identification and communication, are not much more than reference points. The organization of all forms of life, in their almost infinite variety, into a system of relationships based on a sound and consistent anatomical and physiological scale of resemblances and differences had never before been achieved in the history of man. The Greeks had made some beginnings in this direction, but had not gotten very far. Other attempts had been flawed by the inconsistent use of anatomical criteria. One obvious and well-known example is the whale. Because he lived in the sea and swam like a fish, he was regarded as one until modern systematics revealed his mammalian origins.

The branch of biology concerned with systematic classification of organisms owes its development in large measure to the stimulus provided by the Age of Discovery. Before the fifteenth century, biology and zoology, like most sciences, had lain dormant. Some of the beginnings of a science of systematics that the Greeks and their predecessors in Asia and Egypt had initiated had become frozen into a set of traditional dogmas, while the rest had been ignored or forgotten during the Dark Ages. While medicine, astronomy, physics and chemistry once more became active areas of curiosity and research, zoology remained more or less inert. But as European explorers began to move into previously unknown areas of the world, they brought back as booty all kinds of collections representative of the strange lands and peoples they had encountered. Some of the finest treasures of these alien cultures were carried back to Spain, Portugal and, later, to France and England. Some were presented to the Vatican. Most of the objects of gold and other precious metals were quickly melted down for local currencies and other uses. This loss—of some of the finest art of the Incas and Aztecs for example—produces a shudder in the archeologist and the lover of primitive art today.

Along with these cultural curiosities came collections of plants and animals as well as other samples of the foreign ecologies. Many, if not most, were unknown to European experts. As these objects accumulated, they stimulated a natural interest in their similarities or differences with familiar flora and fauna. Some kind of organization or arrangement was necessary if any sense whatever was to be made of their bewildering and fascinating complexities, their off-beat similarities and their perplexing differences.

During the sixteenth, seventeenth and well into the eighteenth centuries, a very large part of the biological research in European centers of learning and science became concerned with this problem. In many such seats of research, it was the dominant branch of biology. As interest and knowledge grew, it became common for dedicated researchers to make special trips to then remote and little-known areas of the world to search for additional material or to find the clues that the explorer, in his casual and inexperienced collecting, would not have recognized and would therefore have overlooked. By the time of Captain Cook, it had become a regular practice for major exploratory expeditions to take along zoological experts to make collections with the sophistication that the science now required. Cook, himself, was accompanied by the German botanist Forster. And Darwin, on the cruise of the *Beagle*, was taken on for the same purpose, with results that are well known. The list is long and full of distinguished names, frequently immortalized in the scientific nomenclature of their discoveries.

As I have already mentioned, one of the first attempts to arrange all forms of life into an organized system was made by Linnaeus, and it has remained, with all its modifications, refinements, added subdivisions and inevitable corrections, a fundamental work from which one can see all the later changes emerging without destroying its basic concepts.

One of the fundamental assessments Linnaeus made was to place man in the order of Primates, which includes the lemurs, monkeys and apes. This was the first time man had been linked scientifically with these animals. In retrospect, it may seem curious that Linnaeus did not draw what now seems the obvious conclusion, that such classificatory relationships were the by-product of an evolutionary process. But Linnaeus lived a century before the evolutionary concept began to emerge from these systematic studies. Even though his system resembled a tree, with all the leaf-bearing twigs representing the living species connected back branch-by-branch to the trunk itself, he did not see that the branches represented former twigs that in their growth had developed this terminal multiplicity. I presume that Linnaeus simply accepted the traditional creation and did not concern himself with the *why* of his classificatory system.

Although Linnaeus' work became a standard text, I know of no critical evaluation of the effect of his grouping man with the Primates. It appears to have been widely accepted. And although it did not then lead to an evolutionary concept of the origin of man, it must have played a significant role in subconsciously predisposing students to the idea of some kind of relationship between man and the animal kingdom. For, in spite of the shock that Darwin delivered to the religious establishment with his views of man's origins, a surprising number of biologists and zoologists, familiar with the accepted classificatory position of man, were prepared to accept the theory of evolution. Some scientists, notably Louis Agassiz in the United States, rejected it but, on the whole, the great majority were quick to side with Darwin. Maybe we owe an unacknowledged debt to Linnaeus.

After more than a century of tracing the fossil ancestry of man, combined with studies of comparative anatomy, adaptation, primate behavior and other adjunct fields, there are still many unsolved problems; but it has been distinctly encouraging to observe the increasing number of basic insights into the process, with a growing assurance that we are on the right track.

One of the fundamental inferences that we can draw is that the arboreal adaptation of our primate ancestors made it all possible. Without that, man could not have evolved as he is today. No other line of animals provided the potential, for man without the upright posture and grasping, manipulative hand derived from his arboreal lineage is inconceivable. With these acquisitions and the rapidly developing brain that was in large measure stimulated by them, he was enabled to pursue the course he has followed. Although each animal adapting and evolving has several alternative courses open for further differentiation, nevertheless, its initial equipment and the adaptive process limit the choice, if we can unscientifically call it that.

There are many other animals that have taken completely to an arboreal way of life. But, for one reason or another, they have not all followed the same pattern of anatomical adaptation as the primates. As a result, although their skill in the trees may be every bit as great, or greater, than that of the primates, they could never evolve in the same direction. One of the primates' distinctive tree-climbing mechanisms is the use of the hand to grasp branches, either crawling and hopping along their length, or jumping and swinging from them. This involves using the fingers for taking hold, with the thumb opposite them to complete the encirclement. This kind of grasp for arboreal locomotion was possible because the primitive primates took to the trees very early in their career. They had inherited the pentadactyl, or five-fingered, hand traditional in land-living vertebrates, and it had not undergone any changes that would have made it unsuitable for the grasping technique they adopted. Mammals that took to the trees after some preliminary adaptations to ground locomotion found themselves with padded paws and reduced digits, and no longer able to grasp a branch or even a twig. Necessarily, they had to adapt to tree climbing by developing claws instead of the nails usually found on primate hands and feet. All one has to do is watch a squirrel or chipmunk nimbly running up a wide tree trunk, digging its claws into the bark, to see how different a performance this is.

Two by-products of the primate form of arboreal locomotion were a flexible body and a semi-erect posture. The first was essential in a milieu where one's support varied with every movement, and the latter developed from the necessity of reaching out and often overhead when progress was upward. As a result, primates, particularly the more developed ones, often tend to sit up even when in a relaxed state. There was, of course, much variation among the primates in the style of this basic locomotion and consequently in their anatomical adaptations. Some of the more primitive forms crawled in a fairly pronograde position with their limbs, fore and aft, about equal in length. Some South American monkeys developed grasping tails by which they could swing from bough to bough. The anthropoid apes became brachiators, swinging by their arms for distances as great as thirty to forty feet. This style of locomotion emphasized the mechanical efficiency of long arms, particularly the forearm, in using muscular energy. As a result, the apes have relatively short legs and arms that, in some, can easily reach the ground even when they are standing fully erect. This bodily proportion, so different from man's, is one of the arguments that the hominid line could not have branched off from the fully developed brachiating apes, as was thought earlier. When such apes, like the gorilla, take to the ground, they tend to use their extremely long arms as additional support in walking and thus would be unlikely to move into a fully upright, two-legged gait. Although this reasoning is widely accepted and may well be one of the decisive factors for eliminating any of the developed brachiating apes as candidates for an ancestral role to mankind, some observations of living apes raise certain problems. For example, the chimpanzee has frequently been seen to walk erect in his native environment, despite his elongated arms. And I, myself, have seen Meshie, a female chimpanzee raised by Harry Raven as a member of his family, walk upright for considerable periods of time, even though her gait in this position was somewhat awkward and her long arms posed something of a problem. But still, I tend to agree with those who favor the hominids' descent from an apelike line that was not so fully committed to brachiation as are the modern apes.

Another consequence of the brachiating specialization was a tendency for the size of the thumb to be reduced. One can easily appreciate that in swinging from one branch to another ten or twenty feet away it would be a distinct advantage to have the hand sufficiently elongated and reinforced to act as a kind of hook that would not give way at the wrist under the enormous force of the impact and weight of the accompanying body. Also, a long thumb, like our own and those of many nonbrachiating primates, would be a hazard to the hand functioning as a hook since it might easily deflect it and cause the brachiator to miss his mark. As a result, the thumb in these apes is not only relatively short, but is actually reduced in size. This has not robbed the apes completely of an opposable thumb with its ability to pick up objects, but it has forced them to use their hands for manipulation in a somewhat different way than we do.

Another potentially significant result of adaptation to an arboreal life is the effect it can have on the sensory dependence of an animal separated from the stimuli it might encounter on the ground and by which it would direct its actions. In general, ground-living animals are largely, if not entirely, dependent upon their senses of smell and hearing. Other senses play a role, but these are dominant. The dog, running with assurance through a field, with his nose close to the ground, is following clues to which he is especially sensitive and which would mean nothing to us even if we could smell them.

For the primates, living mostly in trees and removed by, let us say, forty or fifty feet from the ground, nasal acuity would be less important in tracking food or in sensing danger. The sense of smell, therefore, became less dominant and was largely replaced by vision as one of the major sensory channels. More than sixty years ago, Wood Jones, a distinguished English anatomist, was one of the first to attribute to this change in the primates an important role in the development of their brains, which show in the course of their evolution a progressive increase and more complex structure.

The importance of vision in these arboreal animals was also reflected in the notably increased and even new functions it came to possess. The first primates, like most ground-living mammals, probably did not have either stereoscopic or color vision. The former imparts a heightened sense of the position of objects in space, an ability of the greatest importance to anyone moving nimbly in the trees. Walking on the ground, you don't have to look carefully for each step you take. If you did, progress would be immeasurably slowed down and speed, when needed, would be virtually impossible. All of us ground-walkers, two- or four-footed, can take it pretty much for granted that solid ground is under foot. There can, of course, be exceptions and our faith may be betrayed with an accident, but they are rare. In the trees, this footing that we take for granted does not exist. Branches twist in all directions, and it would be fatal at considerable heights to assume that one will be where it should be without looking. But looking is not enough unless you have acute spatial perception. This ability is greatly enhanced when the fields of vision of the two eyes overlap and produce stereoscopy. In most land animals the eyes are placed so far apart and, often, with their planes of vision so divergent that such overlapping of the fields of vision does not occur. It can take place when the eyes lie in the same plane, with the lines of vision more or less parallel, and when they are close enough to produce the overlap. Anyone who has had to depend on one eye temporarily knows how the height of a step or a curb suddenly becomes a problem, until one subconsciously learns to adjust to the loss of the sharp sense of position and space that our stereoscopic vision gives us.

As we follow the evolutionary adaptations of the primates, it is possible to observe a progressive movement of the eye sockets, and therefore the eyes, to a more frontal position. As a result, they become more closely set and aligned in the same plane, making stereoscopic vision possible. This suggests that the ability to leap from branch to branch and the highly developed brachiation of the apes may be linked with this progressive enhancement of stereoscopic vision.

Color vision, which we take for granted and generally assume to be characteristic of all animal life, is actually limited in its distribution. Some insects and some animals have it, but many do not and see the world around them in shades of gray. If you are used to it, as we were with the black-and-white movies, you can live with it, but after color comes it can only seem a deprivation to be without it. Exactly why the primates acquired color vision is not altogether clear. Perhaps an ability to distinguish color is important in an arboreal life, although the earlier primates did without it. One could, of course, say the same of stereoscopic vision, but this apparently developed much earlier and permitted the greater agility we can observe in the higher primates.

Why any of the primates gave up their arboreal existence and took to living on the ground again, as their remote mamalian ancestors had done millions of years before, is thus far a matter of speculation. When one considers how well-adapted they were for tree life, taking to the ground would seem a limitation of their skills and therefore enough of a disadvantage to have discouraged any commitment to such a new form of life and locomotion. Moreover, the primates may have stayed in the trees because of the protection it afforded them from predators less agile than themselves in ascending the heights or in leaping or swinging from tree to tree.

Yet at several stages of their evolution, some did take to the ground. Among the Old World monkeys—the cercopithecids—several species have become terrestrial. The best-known are the baboons, the macaques and the mandrills. Of the anthropoid apes, the gorilla has become largely ground-living, rarely using the trees for locomotion. And, of course, this is true of our own hominid ancestor. The new method of locomotion adopted can be attributed to the anatomical attributes each brought to its new habitat. The baboons and their related cercopithecids have reverted in a curious and fascinating way to features characteristic of ground-living mammals, but in a manner influenced by their previous arboreal adaptations. For example, baboons run on the ground on all four limbs but have not developed pads, paws or hooves. Although their primate hands and feet have lost some of their previous flexibility, they have retained their five digits with opposable thumbs. Living close to the ground as they do, their sense of smell has again become highly significant, and the nose has become enlarged and snoutlike to provide space for the more complex nasal structure associated with their enhanced sensitivity. Yet the muzzle, face and teeth retain the basic primate pattern.

The baboon's adoption of four-legged locomotion on the ground suggests that the primate lineage from which it branched off was still pretty much committed to a horizontal form of locomotion in the trees, creeping or crawling on all fours but using the hands and feet for grasping. Taking to the ground would then be simply substituting one kind of support for another.

The gorilla's ground locomotion is quite different. Although he often stands erect to look around him or to beat his chest or let out a roar, his normal gait is semi-erect with the major weight of his body on his legs and feet and his arms assisting in the locomotion. With the extremely long arms of a brachiating ape, he can easily reach the ground to maintain his body in a semi-erect position. In fact, it is partly due to these long arms that the gorilla cannot, even if he wished to, adopt the fully horizontal posture of the baboon. And it may also have been a factor discouraging fully erect posture since arms as long as these could be something of a hindrance in such a position.

An interesting side light on the gorilla's method of locomotion is that the hands do not touch the ground with the palms flat as in the case of the baboon. Instead, the gorilla uses his knuckles, with the wrists stiff. Some observers attribute this to his former adaptation as a brachiator, when the hooklike hand and a stiff wrist were a great advantage. Endowed with these characters when coming to the ground, the gorilla could use his hand only by knuckling since the wrist had become too rigid to permit bending the palm down flat. Incidentally, this is another feature, common in the present-day apes, that some scholars have used as an argument against deriving man's ancestors from an evolved brachiating ape. Apparently the gorilla took the right road but a little bit too late and ended up as *Homo manqué.*

If anything is indisputable in the human evolutionary line it is that man's hominid ancestors, on taking to the ground, began to walk on two legs with their bodies held upright. If they did not begin to do so at once, it could not have been long after. If they had become accustomed and initially adapted to any other form of ground locomotion, it is most unlikely that they would have shifted later to their present stance. Of course, in the beginning this posture was not as fully achieved or as natural as it was to become later as specific anatomical changes developed that made erect posture increasingly efficient. Various muscles had to acquire the power to hold the torso erect above the pelvis. Some of these became so large and powerful that they began to protrude as the buttocks, a feature typical of the human species and anatomically necessary if upright posture is to be maintained. That this distinctly human attribute has come to fill the eye of the male (the Greeks had a word for it—*callipygous*) does not mean, as some writers have suggested, that it owes its origin to sexual selection. This would imply that the girls with biggest buttocks, having the greatest appeal, would produce more babies than the less well endowed, and thus their offspring, gifted with their mothers' genes for bigger and better rear ends, would outnumber the less fortunate. If this were true, we should by now have gone way beyond our present standards.

As one examines in detail the bones and muscles of the human body, the effect of upright posture is found to permeate virtually every part of it, from the feet to the head. All these changes were, of course, a long time in developing as they are today, but most of them were far advanced relatively early in the hominid evolution—in fact, well before various other traits we think of as distinctly human.

Two questions especially occur to one at this point. Why did man's ancestors take to the ground if they were already so well adapted to the trees? And why did they adopt upright posture when, as we have seen, other primates following the same route did not? The fossil record on the first question is not, and perhaps never can be, specific. Some have argued that as a result of fluctuations in climate, belts of more limited rainfall had invaded the heavily forested homeland of our primate ancestors, eliminating the trees or thinning them out to produce a savannah-like country. Under such circumstances, the primate dwellers in the former forests could either follow the retreat of their ecological niche, or they could learn to live with the change by taking to ground living. Others have suggested that our primate ancestors had discovered sources of food on the ground, seeds and small game that their flexibility permitted them to utilize, and that this tended to keep them where the larder was.

A recent variation of the food stimulus, advanced in a book by Miss Elaine Morgan, *The Descent of Woman*, offers the possibility that our ancestors, having somehow discovered the rich treasures of marine food, began exploiting watery environments and, to keep from gulping the water, were forced to stand erect, thus acquiring upright posture. Here, obviously, is a field for imaginative reconstruction, which of course can be useful only if supported by some hard facts.

That man's ancestors adopted erect posture, or something approaching it, when they did finally take up a terrestrial existence has a number of implications. First of all, they must have branched off from a line that had not yet become specialized brachiators. Yet they must have reached a degree of adaptation to erect or semi-erect posture beyond that of the monkey ancestors of the baboon. This has led some students to infer that the hominid line took off from a higher primate group that had already achieved such a posture in the initial stages of brachiation, but before the full effects of this mode of locomotion, had irreversibly closed the door to the two-legged gait on the ground.

It is significant that this form of terrestrial locomotion appears to have been well established in the *Australopithecines*. When their first cranial fragments were uncovered, it became evident that these creatures were bipedal and erect. This could be readily determined from the position of the foramen magnum, the opening in the base of the skull through which the spinal cord passes to connect the complex, branching nerve system with the brain. In a pronograde, four-legged mammal, this opening is at the very posterior of the skull, at the point where it is attached to the spinal column. In a fully upright man, the foramen magnum has necessarily moved forward and downward until it lies, not at the back of the skull, but toward the middle of its base, because in upright posture the skull is balanced on top of a vertical spinal column. Thus, by examining the position of the foramen magnum of any primate fossil, one can immediately estimate the degree of adaptation to erect posture.

The pelvic region in the human skeleton has also undergone dramatic alterations in shape, relationship of parts, joints and other details, all reflecting the special stresses and resulting accommodations that upright posture involves. There can be no mistaking a pelvis adapted to the human gait for one adjusted to a semi-erect or pronograde locomotion. Similarly, the form and muscular markings of the leg bones clearly reflect this adaptation.

In all these anatomical areas, the *Australopithecines* had come a long way from their primate precursors. They were distinctly manlike and obviously had been adapting to an erect gait for a long time. They were, in fact, far closer to human standards in this respect than they were in the development of the brain. Thus, this evidence not only confirms the now-general conclusion that these extinct hominids are in the direct line leading to *Homo sapiens*, or closely related to it, but also highlights the decisive role that erect posture played in determining its course of development.

Two other features require some comment: hand and brain. Indeed, without them and their interplay it is inconceivable that man as he is today could ever have evolved.

The grasping, manipulative hand, with the opposable thumb that adds immeasurably to its skill and efficiency, is a good example of a structure adapted and evolved for one purpose but ending up performing quite a different function. This new function, the making and use of artifacts, and eventually a complex technology, has a significance in human evolution that cannot be overemphasized. It is fundamental. Thus man is unique in now finding himself adapting not so much to the natural environment, which gave him and all his fellow beings their form, character and potentiality, but to an artificial environment that he himself has created and may change and modify.

All this was initially made possible by the hand functioning under the control of a brain that became increasingly complex with the evolution of man. But the hand as a first-class instrument is, of course, only as ingenious as the brain that governs and controls it and that thinks up new uses to which it can be applied.

At the *Australopithecine* and *Homo habilis* stage, however, the interplay of hand and brain had not yet produced a high level of technology. What evidence there is reveals a very simple kind of technique employed in making what are known as pebble tools. These are crudely fashioned but recognizable as deliberate manufactures, which distinguishes them significantly from the stray stones or sticks that apes are known to use as tools. One might be inclined to infer from such evidence that the hominids at this stage had attained some but not an impressive degree of intellectual capacity above the anthropoid ape endowment. But perhaps this step in the direction of a human technology different from any other should not be underestimated, simple as it is. Such first tentative steps in a new development may well reflect fundamental cerebral changes of great importance.

The only other method of assessing the brain development of these fossil hominids is by examining natural or artificial casts of the interior of the skull. This, however, is beset with difficulties since only size and certain surface impressions that the brain makes on the inner bony layer of the skull are available as direct evidence. Nevertheless, with considerable ingenuity certain critical determinations have been made, and some conclusions can apparently be drawn from them. Professor Ralph L. Holloway of Columbia University, who has devoted much skill and effort to this research, has concluded that the brains of both the *Australopithecines* and *Homo habilis* were clearly hominid. In brain size alone, however, the *Australopithecines*, both *africanus* and *robustus*, had not yet reached a level in absolute size much beyond the gorilla.

The *robustus* variety had an average cranial capacity slightly more than 500 c.c., and *africanus*, slightly less. These, Holloway points out, when measured against their small body size compared with the gorillas, are far more impressive than they might at first appear since there is a correlation between brain and body size. *Australopithecines* could be expected to have a considerably larger cranial capacity if they were as large as modern man or a gorilla.

Homo habilis, who was contemporaneous with the *Australopithecines* and is regarded by some experts as distinct from them, had an even larger brain, averaging slightly over 600 c.c.; and the fossil recently discovered by Richard Leakey in East Africa, the status of which is still under study, had a still larger brain although also contemporary with the *Australopithecines* and *Homo habilis*.

But perhaps more critical in assessing the cerebral development of these fossil hominids are the regional developments and surface arrangements of their brains, which can be discerned from casts of the interior of the skull. In Holloway's opinion, the *Australopithecines* and *Homo habilis* have patterns that are characteristically hominid and distinct from those found in other primates.

The big question then becomes: What stimulated the growth of the brain, and why did it come after the early hominids had adapted to a terrestrial existence? For although the primates on the whole, and progressively in the course of their evolution, reveal a very respectable development of the brain, making them in this respect one of the distinctive orders of mammals, none ever approached the human level.

The answer is at present not easily provided. Some students have suggested that social developments among these early hominids played an important role. Another possibility I have already stressed is the use of the hand in technological innovations. This, through a kind of feedback system, might have been very critical in selecting for superior ability, which in turn would have advanced cultural and technological achievements to continue the selective process.

This endowment of hand and brain, destined to direct the course of human evolution, came with the early hominids, but it was in the beginning just a potentiality. Only as the opportunities to use the tool became increasingly significant could the interplay between brain and hand continue and lead on to the results we may observe around us. Had these first hominids simply employed natural objects that came to hand, as their ape cousins did, nothing much would have developed. It was only as they began to make tools deliberately and fashion them into distinctly more effective instruments that this technology, simple as it was, slowly began to exert a selective pressure that favored the brighter and more capable of the primitive hominids.

Language is conceivably of the most importance as one of the determining factors in brain growth. I have already referred to this in discussing the probability that Peking man could use language. But that the early hominids had already acquired any degree of linguistic ability seems from present evidence unlikely. This would therefore suggest that language was not yet a significant factor in their cerebral advancement. To what, then, can we attribute the notable increase of brain size in *Homo erectus?* Although his technology had certainly become more sophisticated, it had scarcely reached a level that would seem to demand a major advance in the neurological complexity of the brain. Similarly, from what we can infer of his social structure there is little to suggest that this provided a selective pressure that would account for the phenomenon. But a steadily developing mechanism of communication leading to the eventual emergence of language with a complex interplay of symbols and abstractions would require not only an increase in the neural equipment of the brain but very possibly a reorganization of some of its structures.

This relationship between language and brain development is still far from being thoroughly understood, but of all the possible influences that might have led to the expansion of the brain in *Homo erectus*, no other stimulus than language is adequate to explain it.

6

———

BELATED NEWS

For over thirty years the fossil relics of Peking man, one of the significant stages in human evolution, had been missing —lost, discarded or stolen. No one really knew what had happened to them, although a variety of stories had become current immediately after their disappearance. Some of these accounts were soon abandoned since they clearly did not fit the known facts. Others, however, continued to circulate even though there was little or no proof of their validity. Even years after the event, new stories continued to surface. On March 22, 1951, for example, *The New York Times* published Dr. Pei's charge that the Japanese had indeed seized the two cases containing the fossils and shipped them to Tokyo, where they were found by the Americans when they occupied Japan at the end of World War II. Pei went on to claim that General MacArthur's headquarters had then sent them on to the United States, where he insisted they were now located. In the light of Dr. Pei's own publication, written before the People's Republic of China took over the Chinese Mainland, this story seems rather odd. For the most part, however, the people intimately concerned with this record of man's past had become reconciled to its disappearance or, at least, had accepted it as a tragic fate for such precious data. Little or nothing much had been done to follow through on the rumors that had reached them. Dr. Weidenreich, who had devoted more than a decade of his life to an unremitting study of the fossils, tried on several occasions to persuade State Department officials in Washington to take some action in following the known leads, but he got nowhere in his efforts.

After his death in 1948, there was no one with his commitment and drive to keep up the pressure that might have led to a clearer knowledge of the circumstances surrounding the loss and to the possibility of recovering some or all of the fossils. The only exception that I can document was Dr. Pei's search in places where he thought they might have been lost or hidden. With the establishment of the People's Republic of China and the breaking off of relations with the United States, the situation became hopeless.

Then one morning in April of 1971, almost thirty years after the loss, Dr. Walter Fairservis came into my office with an air of excitement to announce that he had just received a telephone call from a Mr. Herman Davis. Davis worked in the office of Dr. William T. Foley, a prominent heart specialist in New York City, and was calling on Dr. Foley's behalf. Dr. Foley, apparently in preparing the memoirs of his career serving in the Marine Corps in China, had come across Fairservis' name in the records in Washington. These were concerned with Weidenreich's efforts in 1946–47 to have Fairservis assigned to the task of searching out the facts that might have led to the recovery of the fossils, and Dr. Foley now hoped to get from Fairservis the names of others who had been involved in the correspondence. From the conversation with Davis, Fairservis had reached the conclusion that Dr. Foley knew something about the loss of the Peking fossils that the rest of us did not know. He wanted to report this to me at once, knowing my deep professional concern over the fate of the fossils and being aware in particular of my personal involvement in the matter through my close association with Weidenreich and his efforts. And he knew of my implication as the alleged custodian of the fossils, for I had been publicly charged with harboring them.

As Fairservis no doubt anticipated, I reacted immediately by calling Dr. Foley's office to make an appointment to see him and Davis. Davis answered, and from his brief account on the telephone, I knew at once that I was on the trail of some critical information. Though where it might lead was, of course, unpredictable at this point, it was obvious that I had to follow it. We made arrangements to meet, and they also agreed to permit me to tape their stories in their own words.

I distinctly recall the feeling of excitement I experienced as, clutching my tape recorder, I went across town to East 68th Street, where Dr. Foley's office was situated. When I arrived, Dr. Foley was occupied, but Davis was free and we retired to an unoccupied office to talk.

Essentially, Davis's story was as follows: In the autumn of 1941, he was a pharmacist's mate in the U.S. Navy, stationed at Camp Holcomb in Chingwangtao, which was the port for Tientsin. In his charge were seventeen marines who formed a medical unit under the command of Dr. Foley, a Marine medical officer who was himself living in Tientsin.

At that time, conditions in China had become distinctly ominous. As an expansion of Japanese military activity was anticipated momentarily, it was decided to transfer the entire Marine detachment stationed in the Peking area—which included Tientsin and Chingwantao—to the Philippines, where we were strongly based. The departure was scheduled for December 8, on the S.S. *President Harrison*.

Late in November, Davis received word from Dr. Foley that some footlockers labeled with his name were being sent to Camp Holcomb from Peking. These, he was told, were personal baggage and were to be carefully guarded and held for shipment on December 8. Shortly thereafter, a freight train from Peking pulled into the siding at the camp, and Dr. Foley's boxes were unloaded. Davis stacked them in his own room for safety, along with other baggage that had been made ready for shipment.

Davis related that when he awoke on the morning of December 8 (December 7, New York time), he looked out his window and discovered that the camp was surrounded by Japanese soldiers. Six Japanese planes were circling overhead and there was a Japanese gunboat in the harbor. Davis may well have been somewhat startled by this turn of events, but I suspect it was not unexpected.

The Japanese called on Davis and his companions to surrender, but, in the tradition of the Marines, they at first refused and were preparing to resist. In any event, Davis told me that he immediately mounted a machine gun on the pile of boxes in his room and began getting ready to shoot it out—but a call was put through at once to the top command in Peking to report the situation. Davis was ordered not to offer resistance since the situation was hopeless, but to surrender.

The Japanese straight away placed the Marines under arrest. Before herding them off to Tientsin for temporary imprisonment, they permitted each man to pack a single bag of personal belongings. The rest of the luggage, including the footlockers sent from Peking in Dr. Foley's name, remained behind, apparently for inspection, and was then to be forwarded to Tientsin. A week or two later, the boxes of the Marines were delivered to them in their prison camp at Tientsin. Davis described their condition as a mixed-up jumble of personal effects. It was abundantly clear that the enlisted men's boxes had been opened, ransacked and the contents replaced helter-skelter. Davis reported that when he sorted out the mess, he was convinced that the Japanese had pilfered some of the men's belongings and felt sure that, had they found any fossils, they would have discarded them in the vicinity of the camp, unaware of their importance and ignorant of the Japanese authorities' overwhelming desire to locate them.

Dr. Foley then gave me his version of the fate of the

footlockers. Some explanatory additions I have derived from other sources.

The boxes bearing Dr. Foley's name were not sent to Davis and his companions in the prison camp at Tientsin, but were delivered to Dr. Foley, himself. His involvement with these boxes dated from an order he had received from Colonel Ashurst, his commanding officer at Peking. The officials at the Peking Union Medical College, Dr. Houghton and Mr. Bowen, and their Chinese colleagues at the Cenozoic Research Laboratory had, after prolonged and painful discussion, decided to remove the fossils from China to the United States for safekeeping until hostilities had ceased and conditions were favorable for their return. There had never been any intention to transfer them permanently, for this was distinctly contrary to the policy of the China Board of the Rockefeller Foundation, which had financed the excavations. On consulting with the Marine Corps, it was decided to entrust the fossils to Dr. Foley, who was also a Research Fellow at the Medical College. Having completed his three-year term of duty in China, he was to join the rest of the Marines in their planned departure for Manila on December 8 but would continue on from there to New York. Thus he was the obvious and appropriate choice as guardian of the precious fossils on their journey to a safe haven. The footlockers containing the fossils were labeled as Foley's personal luggage and were the boxes that he had alerted Davis to receive at Camp Holcomb and guard with care.

Dr. Foley informed me that he had seen some of the fossils being packed in large glass jars and placed in the footlockers. However, Mrs. Taschdjian, who was Dr. Weidenreich's assistant and took part in the packing of the fossils, did not, when I spoke to her somewhat later, recall the use of glass jars. Her recollection was that the fossils had been carefully bedded in loose packing material. Although just how the fossils were packed may be a matter of small importance, I was somewhat puzzled by the discrepancy. Since Dr. Foley had not participated personally in the packing, I was inclined to attribute his description to hearsay. But curiously enough I found in the January 4, 1952, issue of *The New York Times* a story on the loss of the fossils in which the reporter, Charles Grutzner, states, "...one account is that the bones, put in glass jars that were then wadded down in two packing cases, marked as officers' clothing, went on the train with the marines' other baggage." Where the *Times* reporter obtained this description of the packing is not clear, but at about this time J. J. Markey also released to the press a similar description. In my own experience, packing such specimens in glass jars would be rather unusual.

Later in his narrative, Dr. Foley mentioned a footlocker labeled with Colonel Ashurst's name, which he believed had also contained fossils. I have been unable to verify this, however, and Davis made no mention of boxes received in Colonel Ashurst's name. But this may not be of any significance.

On the day that the war broke out—December 8—Dr. Foley also was immediately placed under arrest. He was transferred to the Marine barracks for about a week, but was then permitted to return to his home in the British Concession. At first he was allowed semi-diplomatic status, which gave him freedom to move around the city, though not beyond its limits. This lasted for about a week, and while still enjoying this priviliged arrest, he received his boxes from Camp Holcomb, those containing the fossils sent from Peking as well as his personal luggage, apparently unopened and intact. I asked Dr. Foley why the boxes bearing his name were delivered in this fashion while those belonging to the other Marines from Camp Holcomb had been opened and rifled and their contents mixed up. He replied that when he opened his personal boxes he had found that several skulls he had kept as anatomical specimens and a Chinese Buddha figure were missing. He had not opened the footlockers assigned to him from Peking. The fact that the boxes had been sent to him instead of to the Marines he attributed to the customary Japanese courtesy and respect for rank.

Faced as he was with the prospect of an extended internment (which, in fact, began shortly and lasted for four years), Dr. Foley decided to distribute the Peking footlockers to various depositories for safekeeping. Some went to the Swiss Warehouse and the Pasteur Institute, both in Tientsin, and some were placed in the care of two Chinese friends on whom he felt he could rely.

A discrepancy appears at this point which may be due to the tricks of memory after thirty years. At a minimum, there would have been four boxes distributed in the fashion Dr. Foley describes. And to this number one would have to add a fifth—the footlocker bearing Colonal Ashurst's name, which also, according to Dr. Foley, contained fossils. But Mrs. Taschdjian firmly recalled that only two footlockers were used for packing the fossils. Dr. Pei, in his account, also specifically refers to only two boxes. Considering that the fossils were mostly fragments of cranial bones, teeth and some long bones, it would seem that two boxes would have been adequate to contain the lot. It is, of course, possible that more than the Peking man relics was eventually packed for shipment out of the country. It is known that the so-called "upper cave material" was also removed and that various records and other pertinent matter may have been included for transferral out of the country. In addition, one account refers to the inclusion of "most valued documents" from the U.S. Embassy.

When Colonel Ashurst, Dr. Foley and their fellow officers lost their diplomatic status they were declared prisoners of war. They were all shipped to a prison camp near Shanghai, where they took their luggage, including the one footlocker that Dr. Foley said carried Colonel Ashurst's name. For some reason I cannot determine, Ashurst was convinced, according to Dr. Foley, that this footlocker contained the most important of the fossils. As far as I know, the Colonel did not participate in the packing of the boxes and, judging from his reputation, he was scarcely one to be deeply interested in relics of fossil man. He was a sportsman with little concern for the artistic or scientific treasures of China. Yet Dr. Foley emphasized Ashurst's sense of responsibility for the safety of this particular box. It may well be that he had been strongly impressed by Dr. Houghton or by our embassy with the importance of his mission in seeing that the fossils reached safety.

When Ashurst and Foley arrived at the prison camp, they managed to keep this footlocker under their own surveillance and prevent it from being opened and inspected. Subsequently, the group of U.S. Marine officers including Ashurst and Foley was removed to another prison camp at Chung Wan, somewhat nearer Shanghai, they were again successful in protecting the box from routine inspection that such a change of camps might entail.

Then, in June 1945, the prisoners and their effects were transferred once more, this time to Fungtai, near Peking. Once again they somehow managed to save the box, presumably containing the fossils, from inspection. In retrospect, this threefold success seems miraculous, but Dr. Foley was very convincing about the stratagems employed to achieve it.

After all these narrow escapes, it is tragic to have to relate that at the end of the war this box, which had survived so many moves and so many hazards, disappeared with its secrets. According to Dr. Foley, the last he saw of it was when he and Colonel Ashurst parted company, the former being sent to an abandoned iron mine in Northern Japan, and the latter to Hokkaido. There they remained until arrangements could be made to return them to the United States.

Colonel Ashurst died a few years after the war and, as far as I have been able to determine, he left no official report to explain what eventually happened to the footlocker. Neither did Dr. Foley make a report. When I asked him why he had not done so, his explanation seemed reasonable. He was, he said, a junior officer. Colonel Ashurst was his senior and commanding officer. It would not have conformed to military etiquette for him to presume to submit a report that his superior was expected to make. Why Ashurst did not do so is difficult to determine now. One reason may be that it certainly was not part of his normal duties. The whole episode was secretly arranged between the U.S. Embassy and the Peking Union Medical College. He had been called in to help in a non-military capacity, and it is doubtful that he ever received orders from Washington to carry out the role he did. These, of course, are merely surmises but they do help to explain, in part, the curious silence and mystery that surrounded the disappearance of these famous fossils.

I have been able to unearth only one account of this whole affair presumably as Colonel Ashurst saw it. It is in a news story by Robert K. Plumb in *The New York Times* of January 5, 1952, and begins as follows:

> The original remains of prehistoric Peking Man, one of the great treasures of natural history, were last known to be in the possession of Col. William W. Ashurst of the Marine Corps, who commanded the marine detachment at the American Embassy at Peiping [Peking] when it was captured by the Japanese on December 7, 1941.

Plumb goes on to say that

> Colonel Ashurst, now a retired brigadier general living in the South, said the relics were given to him personally by Dr. Henry B. Houghton, an American who was in 1941 president of the Peiping Union Medical College. His instructions, Colonel Ashurst said, were to handle the bones as "secret" material. He did not open the boxes, but was informed that they contained the remains of Peking Man. . . . At the insistence of the Chinese Dr. Houghton took the packed relics to Colonel Ashurst. They were loaded on a special train for Chingwangtao . . . Colonel Ashurst said.

The train left Peiping at 5 A.M. December 5 guarded by
nine marines. It arrived safely at Chingwangtao 200
miles away. There it was to wait for the *President Harrison*, steaming north from Shanghai.

In the meantime the Japanese struck at Pearl Harbor
and within a few hours all Americans in North China
were captured. The Embassy, its marine detachment
and all officers, including Colonel Ashurst, were taken
at Peiping. The liner *Harrison*, grounded to save her
from the enemy, was later refloated and repaired by the
Japanese and still later on their first voyage with her
was sunk by a United States submarine.

The train, with cargo intact, was captured at Chingwangtao, Colonel Ashurst said.

This story clearly does not agree with Mr. Davis' specific recollection of removing the boxes and storing them in
his own room. But since Colonel Ashurst was in Peking, he
might have been misinformed or not informed at all.

Plumb continued the story as he received it from
Ashurst:

The nine-man marine guard was sent back to Peiping
within a few days and Colonel Ashurst with 250 men
of his North China command were eventually sent to
prisoner-of-war camps in Japan. The Colonel was released by American troops on September 12, 1945.

There is no mention here of any sojourns in prison
camps in China before being sent off to Japan. But this is
understandable in an abbreviated newspaper account. More
puzzling, however, is the conclusion of Colonel Ashurst's
story as reported by Mr. Plumb:

Burdened with responsibility for his captured troops,
Colonel Ashurst was delayed in learning what happened
to the train. He found out the Japanese took millions of

rounds of ammunition from it and must have gone through everything aboard.

"Perhaps they found the remains and just threw them away," he said, "like canned foods. The Japanese had no use for our foods they captured so they just dumped them off the train.

"The Peking relics must not have looked like much. I hardly realized what they were. Maybe the Japanese just kept what was useful to them at the time and threw everything else away."

Obviously, Davis' account would seem more dependable since he was present at Camp Holcomb when the boxes arrived and personally had them removed to his room. Colonel Ashurst, on the other hand, was speaking from second-hand information, and his conclusion as to the fate of the boxes would appear less reliable. That the Japanese soldiers may have opened the footlockers they found in Davis' room and discarded the fossils cannot be ruled out from any evidence I have come across, but it seems most unlikely that the event occurred as Colonel Ashurst has described it.

Somewhat more difficult to resolve is the fact that the Colonel makes no mention of guarding the footlocker, presumably containing fossils, throughout his prison sojourns. As Plumb retells his story, Ashurst apparently never saw any of the footlockers containing the fossils after they were placed on the train in Peking to be taken to Camp Holcomb at Chingwangtao.

When I obtained Dr. Foley's story of the loss of the fossils, I decided to publish it in an article for *Natural History*. Although I had not learned the whereabouts of the fossils, I did have a firsthand account of the circumstances leading to their loss, and had at least settled some of the numerous unfounded rumors. I knew that to the scientific world interested in Peking man this account would be of considerable importance.

Before the article appeared in the November 1971 issue of the magazine, I arranged to send some advance copies as a courtesy to the Chinese so that they might be informed of what was now coming to light. The Foreign Secretary of our National Academy of Sciences managed to arrange for their delivery through the kind offices of one of the members of the staff that accompanied Dr. Kissinger on his visit to China.

The publication of the article attracted the attention of the press, and *The New York Times*, which has consistently given considerable notice to episodes in the history of Peking man, published a relatively detailed story covering the major aspects of my article and comments that I delivered at a press conference.

Although I had not heard whether or not my prepublication copies had reached the Chinese, I assumed that they had. That *The New York Times* story received circulation in China appears quite natural now in retrospect. The article, in fact, aroused great interest, and for many weeks I received requests for copies from scholars around the world.

After the initial excitement, however, things quieted down once more. I had hoped I might receive an indication from China that paleontologists or anthropologists there would be interested in pursuing whatever leads Dr. Foley's story provided. But all was silence. After all, it was at this moment that sensitive diplomatic negotiations were taking place, and it seemed an inappropriate time either to hear from China on a matter of this kind or, indeed, to pursue it myself. In any event, I had become more or less resigned that nothing further relating to Peking man was in the immediate offing.

7

THE SEARCH BEGINS AGAIN

About six months after I published "The Strange Unfinished Saga of Peking Man," I received a telephone call early in the summer of 1972 from a man unknown to me. He was Mr. Christopher Janus, just returned from China. It was clear that he was excited about Peking man and had some news to communicate to me. He suggested that we meet for lunch. The story he related to me was as follows.

Mr. Janus, a broker and businessman in Chicago, had founded some years ago an organization that he named The Greek Heritage Foundation. This institution was designed to organize and arrange cultural trips to various parts of the world containing important relics of ancient art and architecture of interest, or where other aspects of the cultures of the past survived. Each year a party of interested people was assembled from all over the country and taken on a three or four–week tour of the selected area. Previously, Mr. Janus told me, they had visited the Near East, Greece and South America. It had occurred to him while President Nixon and Dr. Kissinger were conferring with the Chinese, and the prospects of détente had become bright, that a cultural visit to China would be highly attractive to many Americans, and that if the Greek Heritage Foundation could manage to arrange one it would be a most desirable venture.

In pursuit of this plan, he made a personal exploratory visit to China in May 1972. While he was in Peking discussing the proposed arrangements with Chinese officials, he heard of a new museum recently installed at Chou Kou Tien. I gathered that at that time Mr. Janus was not very familiar with the story of Peking man, if indeed he knew anything about its scientific background. But the opening of a new museum near enough to Peking may have attracted his interest as a possible addition to the tour itinerary.

While he was visiting the museum, Janus told me, he met its director, who very quickly launched into an account of the tragic loss of the fossil relics. And then, with considerable passion and insistence, pleaded with Mr. Janus to get the Americans to help recover these treasures. It is somewhat difficult to interpret exactly what he meant by this. Possibly, he was merely suggesting that American scientists backed by American money could help. But in that case, one cannot but wonder why Chinese scientists who were on the spot, so to speak, where the fossils disappeared could not do as much if not more than any foreigners could. On the other hand, he may have been implying that, in some way unknown to the scientific world, some Americans had secretly and illegally made off with them and that they were possibly to be found in the United States or some other place accessible to Americans but not to mainland Chinese. Mr. Janus, not knowing the details of the loss, was in no position to question the director.

The importance of the fossils and their emotional overtones for the Chinese were, however, sharply brought home to Mr. Janus, who determined to do what he could on his return to the United States. At this stage he was not even fully aware of the circumstances surrounding their loss or the conflicting stories that had gained currency. Nor did he have any idea of the strange, perplexing leads, the frustrating interviews, the fruitless trips that he would get into.

One of the first things Janus did immediately after his return was to give an interview to the press on his visit to

China, and to announce that he would pay a reward of $5,000 to anyone providing him with information leading to the recovery of the lost fossils. When I first met Mr. Janus, he had already issued this appeal, and my initial reaction was decidedly negative. I told him that such an announcement, offering so substantial a reward, would inevitably attract a flood of letters and calls from the lunatic fringe.

Moreover, according to the information I had received from Dr. Foley and had just published, it seemed most unlikely that the fossils had been recognized and secreted outside China. For this reason, too, I was pessimistic about this type of strategy. I was more inclined, if the opportunity presented itself, to go to China and with the collaboration of Chinese colleagues retrace the odyssey of the footlockers on the remote chance that the Pasteur Institute or the Swiss Warehouse might still have one or another of the boxes Dr. Foley recalled placing there, tucked away in a remote corner. The debris at Camp Holcomb seemed a less likely spot to explore, but nevertheless, not to overlook any possibility, this too would be a necessary bit of exploration.

When I expressed my doubts about the efficacy of his offer of a reward, Mr. Janus admitted that he had indeed been inundated with several hundred letters from all over the country, many of them weird and obviously not to be taken seriously. He did say, however, that two or three of them had seemed at first glance to be of some interest and that he intended to pursue these a bit further.

After some additional conversation, Mr. Janus explained that, while in Peking, he had arranged a visit for some thirty to forty people under the aegis of The Greek Heritage Foundation. The trip was to take place in October, and I was invited to join the party to explore, if possible, the leads I had obtained from Dr. Foley. I was, of course, eager and delighted at this opportunity and felt that I had a certain responsibility to take whatever action I could. If it led to the recovery of even a small fraction of the fossils, it would be a contribution. And to have been of some aid in restoring them to China, where they belonged, would have given me great pleasure.

Shortly after this first meeting with Mr. Janus, I met him again while he was on a business trip to New York and he told me of a strange adventure he had had. Among the responses to his reward offer there were three that had seemed to be worth pursuing. One came from a former Marine officer and another from a Chinese businessman located in the Wall Street area. Both professed to have some information of importance which might lead to finding the fossils. But the third came via a telephone call, from a lady who said she had the fossils.

Naturally, Mr. Janus was eager to investigate this claim and at once suggested that she meet with him to discuss the matter. He mentioned several convenient places where they could talk privately. But each of them was rejected. Finally, Mr. Janus, somewhat at a loss to name a place that the lady would find suitable, suggested that she select the place. To his surprise, she at once proposed that they meet at the observatory on the 102nd floor of the Empire State Building, at Fifth Avenue and 34th Street in New York City. In spite of the oddity of this choice, Mr. Janus agreed, and a time and day were set for the encounter.

On the appointed time and day, not fully expecting to see his mysterious caller, Janus went to the Empire State Building and rode up to the 102nd floor. This is a well-known overlook that provides a superb panoramic view of New York City and, on a clear day, its rivers, harbor and environs in New Jersey and Long Island. It is a favorite tourist spot and usually there are a number of them there with their cameras.

When Mr. Janus arrived, he found to his surprise that the lady was there. I presume that some clue for mutual recognition had been arranged. He described her as a good-looking woman, apparently in her late forties. The story she told him was essentially this: After the war, her husband, now deceased, had come back from China with a box that he called his "war booty." This box contained the fossils. He had repeatedly emphasized strongly to his wife that it was very dangerous but worth a lot of money. And he had warned her to be very careful to avoid getting into serious trouble on account of them.

The lady now showed Mr. Janus a photograph of the contents of the box to prove that she did indeed have the fossils. Having no knowledge or experience with this kind of material, Mr. Janus was of course unable to recognize whether or not these were in fact the fossils that the mysterious and still anonymous lady claimed. When he related this episode to me, he said that he could see that there was a scattering of bones in the bottom of the box, but this was scarcely proof that any of them were genuine Peking man fossils.

Suddenly, in the middle of their conversation, the lady quickly gathered up her photograph and headed for the elevator almost at a run. Janus described her as if she were in a panic of terror. He followed her as she made off, and as they rode down in the elevator he questioned her about her sudden flight. She said, "Didn't you see those people with a camera? They were about to take a picture of me." The people she referred to were the tourists normally found on the observation floor of the Empire State Building. That they had a camera and were about to take shots of the spectacular view would be a natural expectation. But apparently the lady had been thoroughly conditioned by her husband, and was obviously in terror, suspecting hidden maneuvers or dangerous plots all around her. The appearance of a camera in the hands of an innocent tourist could well have seemed to her to be a cover-up for getting evidence that might be used against her.

After some further conversation with Mr. Janus while descending from the heights, she agreed to call him up in a few days and continue their discussion. But on reporting this episode to me, Mr. Janus had not yet had word from the lady. He was at this time, in my opinion, not altogether convinced that he was on a hot trail. I agreed that the picture of a box with bony fragments could easily have been faked. And this certainly was a dominant thought in my own reactions to the story.

But one of the startling and, to me, even staggering, aspects of this meeting was the lady's demand for $500,000 before giving up the fossils. This, no doubt, was what she had meant when she spoke of the "war booty" and of her husband's insistence that the bones were extremely dangerous. Subsequently, this story, with the ransom demand, was released to the press and published widely around the country. I almost at once began to feel a considerable uneasiness about this sort of publicity, fearful that it could conceivably lead to a rash of similar events, thefts of other precious fossils with demands of exorbitant sums of money for their release. It was, after all, one successful hijacking of a plane that started a rash of others that has not yet ceased, with increasing exactions and a widening range of exploitation. As a result, I urged that no further mention be made of the ransom in any news releases. And, on one occasion, I was able to convince a responsible reporter to omit any mention of it in an important story he was then writing about the whole affair, although he was already thoroughly familiar with it. And now in my own account of the story of Peking man and the aftermath of his disappearance I find myself faced with the responsibility of suppressing the account of the demands for ransom money or of choosing to tell it as it actually happened, and taking the risks I had previously urged be avoided. My decision has been influenced by several considerations. In the first place, I felt a moral responsibility to relate this account of Peking man and his history before and after his discovery, giving all the information I possessed as a matter of record. The needs of future scholars can never be fully anticipated, and it is incumbent on any responsible writer to present all the facts that may be important. And since the ransom demands were already widely disseminated, my silence would have no appreciable effect.

All this was reinforced by the continued public discussion, even as I write, of the money being offered and asked for to secure the return of the fossils.

Although I was very dubious about the lady's claim of having the bony relics of Peking man in her possession, I did strongly suggest to Mr. Janus that, if and when he spoke to her again, he obtain permission for me to examine them. Or, failing in that, that he secure from her a copy of the photograph she had shown him.

Several weeks elapsed and the mysterious nameless lady made no appearance, nor did she telephone Mr. Janus as she had agreed to do. After waiting a reasonable time, Mr. Janus then inserted a notice in the personal column of *The New York Times* addressed "to the lady who met me in the Empire State Building" and requesting that she call him at a given number.

Within a couple of days, she did call. When it was suggested in the conversation that she permit me to examine the fossils, she apparently did not flatly refuse, but instead raised a number of difficulties that in effect made an examination impossible. When, however, a photograph was requested, she agreed to send one.

Shortly after this, Mr. Janus did receive a copy of the photograph and he then sent me a duplicate of it. It was with considerable interest that I examined the photograph. Although it was far from being a satisfactory image, it did show clearly enough a large, black-looking box with its lid off. The view was directed downward to reveal the contents of the box. Scattered on the bottom were a miscellaneous lot of skeletal bones, none of which looked like the bones of Peking man. In fact, some of them were parts of the skeleton that had never been found at Chou Kou Tien. But in the midst of all this osseous debris there was a skull that attracted my attention. One could see the top of the cranium and, although the photograph left much to be desired for the kind of examination I had hoped to make, the general form and shape of the skull warranted the closest study. I then examined the photograph under a microscope in the hope of being able to discern anatomical details that were not altogether clear to my naked eye. Although the picture did not lend itself to the microscopic enlargement I sought, I was nevertheless able to detect what seemed to me a typical sinanthropic type of brow, with a heavy protruding ridge extending forward just above where the eye sockets would have been had they been visible. Moreover, the occiput was also characteristic of the *Sinanthropine* skull, as was its flat broad appearance seen from above. From my experience, the skull in the box certainly did not look as if it belonged to a *Homo sapiens*. It was tempting to try to identify which of the *Sinanthropus* skulls it resembled most, but under the circumstances it seemed somewhat hazardous to attempt this with so poor a photograph. For the moment, I was convinced that the skull was sufficiently suggestive of a resemblance to Peking man to warrant my encouraging Mr. Janus in his dealings with the lady. I told him I was now of the opinion that she had at least one specimen in the job lot of bones that made her, as well as the skull, interesting enough to pursue.

My comment on the skull was quoted by Mr. Janus in interviews that he gave to the press during these negotiations. None of my professional colleagues questioned my observation. Not having the photograph, they presumably did not feel they were in a position to judge. But I suspect that some of them may have thought I was rash even though I had carefully refrained from a specific identification— simply calling the skull "interesting" and certainly worth a closer inspection than a poor photograph permitted.

A year later, during an international anthropological meeting in Chicago, Mr. Janus gave a talk on his search for the lost fossils to a distinguished audience including some of the leading specialists in human paleontology—experts thoroughly familiar with the *Sinanthropine* data. Unfortunately, I had not been able to attend, but I received reports from both Mr. Janus and my old friend and colleague Professor

William Howells of Harvard about the reactions to the photograph I had studied, which Mr. Janus had shown to him and several others. Howells described how the scattered skeletal bones in the box had at first led him to discount the lady's claim; but when Philip Tobias, a professor of anatomy and well-known authority from South Africa, pointed to the skull, he began to have second thoughts. This led to a careful intensive examination of the one piece that seemed to warrant serious study. Howells now is convinced that it is indeed a *Sinanthropine* skull and is inclined to identify it as Skull Number XI in the Weidenreich nomenclature.

It was in the midst of all the first flurry of newspaper publicity about the mysterious lady and her claims and my assessment of the skull in the box that I received a message one day that a Mrs. Apperson had telephoned my office while I was away. She had left her number in Connecticut with a request that I return the call. For some reason I cannot recall, I was unable to do so immediately. The next day she called again. This time I was able to speak to her.

She began by identifying herself as Mrs. Apperson—a name totally unknown to me. Then she said, "I'm a dowser." My first reaction to this word was the sudden recollection of a neighbor of mine in the country whose dowsing techniques are reputed to be highly successful in finding suitable spots for drilling wells. Mrs. Apperson, however, proceeded to list her membership in some national society of dowsers and other connections with professionals in this field. To establish more fully her identity and authority, she mentioned various dowsing activities in which she had recently been engaged. In particular, she described with considerable enthusiasm her search, along with a group of distinguished fellow dowsers, for traces of Sasquatch in the Maine woods. This is apparently the American counterpart of Yeti, the Abominable Snowman who is supposed to roam the foothills of the Himalayas.

Somewhat puzzled by this recital of her credentials and activities, I asked her: "Why are you calling me? I have nothing to do with dowsing." "But," she replied, "I want to help you find the lady with the fossils." She then proceeded to explain in some detail that she had been very successful in her operations by working on a map. And she suggested that by setting out a map of the New York area she could locate precisely where the mysterious lady was. Rather intrigued but not convinced by all this, I asked her if she used a forked branch of peach or apple wood. "Oh no," she replied, "I use a plastic one." Had I been looking for a likely spot to drill for water, I might have been tempted to use a dowser, since some of my friends claim this inexplicable method for locating underground water has worked for them. But my open-mindedness did not extend far enough to see the rationale for locating on a map the hiding place of the Peking man fossils.

Subsequently, however, some of my colleagues persuaded me to see what Mrs. Apperson's techniques could do, and twice she worked with great concentration and conviction on some maps we provided. The results, alas, were not decisive.

In the meantime, Mr. Janus, in his indefatigable way, was pursuing still another lead. This came from a letter he had received from a Mr. Tze, a Chinese businessman located in the Wall Street area. His communication, apparently stimulated by Mr. Janus' newspaper announcement and offer of a reward, carried enough conviction to make it seem desirable to explore its claims. A meeting was arranged, and Mr. Tze informed Mr. Janus that a friend of his in Taiwan had the fossils and would demand a million dollars for their release. After another meeting or two, Mr. Janus suggested that I call Mr. Tze, who lived in Westchester County in New York.

One evening shortly thereafter, I did call Mr. Tze, but the conversation I had with him led to nothing. He apparently became very alarmed that he was being associated with the missing fossils and immediately denied knowing the man in Taiwan personally. His connection, he kept insisting, was very remote and tenuous. He only knew someone who knew the alleged possessor, but he himself had no direct connection. At one point he became extremely vehement and said, "You are naive. You do not realize the danger involved." He then went on to explain that anyone in possession of the fossils or with direct knowledge of their hiding place would be in danger of his life. My suggestion that we meet to talk over his original claims to Mr. Janus was abruptly dismissed. With some difficulty, I finally managed to close the conversation politely.

While all this was going on, I was anticipating the trip to China under the aegis of The Greek Heritage Foundation. The date of departure was set for October 1972. I had, along with all the other members of the party, filled out the necessary forms for a visa and had made arrangements in my academic commitments to give me the three weeks I needed for the trip. As the departure date neared, word came from Chicago that the visas had not been processed and granted, and that there might therefore be some delay, perhaps a postponement into November. Mr. Janus had called China to try to expedite matters, and a visit to the Chinese government office in Canada had been arranged; but none of these efforts bore fruit, and in the end this trip had to be abandoned. It was then suggested that I join a second tour that had been planned for April 1973. As any devoted gardener would at once agree, this came at a somewhat awkward time, but I was ready to abandon my plans for spring planting in favor of the opportunity to visit China and explore the clues for the missing fossils.

Following this disappointment, I began to consider seriously what previously had occurred to me from time to time, namely that a more determined effort be made to discover who the anonymous lady really was rather than to wait for her unpredictable communications. At one point I had discussed with Mr. Janus that when he spoke to her again he might suggest that she arrange to have a lawyer represent her. I had been informed that she could deposit the fossils in the custody of a legal representative. They would then be, from her point of view, protected and inviolate, for the law of the land states that objects in legal custody cannot be seized. Moreover, Mr. Janus had already been in touch with the State Department on this matter to ascertain what the legalities were from their point of view, and he had been assured that no action would be taken against the lady under the circumstances. In the event that she were willing to do this, I could then presumably have access to the bones in the box in order to examine them for identification, without endangering her anonymity or her possession. As far as I was concerned, it could be determined once and for all whether continued negotiations were desirable or could be completely abandoned with a clear conscience that the real fossils were not involved. The lady did consult a lawyer and Mr. Janus did speak to him, but nothing much came of it.

As an alternative, I began speculating on how I might discover who she was. One thing, at least, seemed certain. She must be a resident of the New York City area. If she came from another part of the country, it would have been inconvenient to arrange a meeting in the Empire State Building. And, moreover, she would have been less likely to see the personal column in *The New York Times*, the channel by which Mr. Janus was able to reestablish communications with her.

Another deduction was equally obvious. Since she had declared to Mr. Janus on their first encounter that her husband had left her the box with explicit warnings of its danger and with strong insistence on its monetary value, she was clearly a widow.

It also seemed likely to me that if the lady had inherited the fossils from her husband, he would have had access to them only if he had been one of the Marines stationed at Camp Holcomb on December 8, 1941, and if the footlockers had indeed reached the camp as Foley and Davis had declared. Dr. Foley had told me that he did not open the footlockers when he finally received them from the Japanese who had seized all the baggage stored at the camp. And it was his belief that they had not been opened. Yet one of his own boxes containing his personal possessions he found had been rifled by the Japanese, and several items removed. Among the many possibilities that had inevitably entered my mind while trying to reconstruct the circumstances surrounding the loss of the fossils, one had repeatedly surfaced. It seemed not improbable to me that one or more of the footlockers from Peking had in fact been opened and some or all of the contents discarded as worthless fragments, since the Japanese soldiers would scarcely be expected to know the significance of these bony fragments or to appreciate their incalculable value. Had they been discarded in this fashion, one of the marines might conceivably have spotted them and recognized them as the fossil remains of Peking man. That a Marine would know the worth of these fossils any more than a Japanese soldier and would rescue them might seem improbable; but, on the other hand, I knew that at least one of the Marines had been shown the fossils. He knew one of the girls who worked at the laboratory and, on one occasion, had been given special dispensation to examine the relics. Since this was an unusual distinction, he would certainly have been inclined to share the experience with his campmates and perhaps to build up the precious nature of the fossils that he had seen. For this reason if no other, I was inclined to suspect that the existence and value of the fossils had been disseminated to some, if not all, the Marines at Camp Holcomb. The principal difficulty with this reconstruction was Davis' account, which seemed to rule out an examination of the boxes while the Marines were still at Camp Holcomb. His story was quite specific that the Marines had been immediately dispatched to prison camp, and that it was only after their departure that the box inspection was made. One other trouble with this hypothesis was the fact that the Marines were allowed, when they left Camp Holcomb, to take only one bag of necessary personal possessions. It is difficult to see how anyone would have concealed so many bones in a bag. Yet, although I could not satisfactorily reenact the circumstances in my own mind, I was prepared to accept tentatively the inference that the anonymous lady's husband had acquired one or more of the fossils.

On the basis of these three items traceable to the anonymous lady, one of her own acknowledgement and the others inferred, I then consulted Mr. Herman Davis, who had originally given me the story of his handling of the footlockers containing the fossils. Mr. Davis had been the sergeant in command at Camp Holcomb and knew intimately every member of the small contingent of Marines that had been stationed and captured at Camp Holcomb. Moreover, the fraternity that developed within this group of men in their overseas station, reinforced by four years of joint imprisonment during the war, had survived after the return to the United States. The Marines of Camp Holcomb have an association today that meets annually in various parts of the country. Davis had remained a loyal member of the group, attended meetings and was in close touch with most of his former comrades.

I asked Mr. Davis if he knew of any of the Marines' having settled in the New York area. He did, and told me the names of a couple of them on Long Island. Were any of these what one might call wheeler-dealers? That amused him. But they were immediately eliminated from my calculations since they were still living and I was looking for someone who had died in the last few years. This, of course, raised the question of whether there were any others to fit the category. One Marine had settled in New Jersey near enough to New York to fit my residence specifications. He also fitted another of my requirements. He had died a few years ago and left a widow.

Mr. Davis' description of this man's proclivities also made it seem a possibility that I was on the right track. However, Davis was not sure of the address, and he referred me to an officer in the Marine Corps in Washington who was at the records office. He, too, had been at Camp Holcomb.

I then wrote to Washington for the widow's address and in due course it was sent to me, along with a copy of a letter written to her about my inquiry. I realized again that, as a sleuth, I was being distinctly amateurish.

Now that I had found a widow of a Marine who had been at Camp Holcomb when the fossils were also there and had survived to return home and settle in the vicinity of New York, I realized that any further investigation would have to be carried out by legal authorities. I was in no position to pursue this matter any further without some risk.

My next step was to call on the State Department in Washington for guidance, and also to urge their action since the whole matter of the lost fossils had international implications. I strongly recommended a search for the anonymous lady, using the clues, if such they were, that I had unearthed or following any leads that one of their own investigators might discover. And I suggested that an FBI agent would be appropriate under the circumstances.

After several conversations, I was finally informed that the FBI's assistance had been arranged and that one of their agents had been assigned to the task. It was clear from these conversations and from previous inquiries made by Mr. Janus that the lady was immune from any legal action and that the search for her now being launched was simply to make contact in order to persuade her to allow me to examine and verify the fossils.

Shortly after this, in January of 1973, FBI agents called on me for whatever information and background I could give them. After several months during which I heard nothing further, I called Washington again and also the FBI agent in New York who was in charge of the investigation. The reports I received were distinctly discouraging. The widow of the Marine living in New Jersey did not fit the description and, as far as I could elicit, provided no evidence that she was the mysterious and anonymous lady. Although the FBI had continued its investigations, talking to many of the former Marines, it had come up with nothing of any promise.

On September 25, 1973, Mr. Janus called from Chicago to alert me once again to the possibility that the tour to Peking might take place after all, and he asked me if I would be prepared to join the party on October 20. When I asked if the visas had arrived, the answer was no. In spite of this, Mr. Janus felt we should be prepared, in case they did. As it turned out once again, the trip did not materialize.

But another matter had come up on which he wanted what assistance I could provide. Some weeks previously, he had received a letter from Gerald L. Beeman, another former Marine from Camp Holcomb, now living in Ohio. He was one of the many Marines with whom Mr. Janus had made contact in his pursuit of the fossils. Mr. Beeman wrote in his letter an account of some recent information he had acquired that proved very exciting to Mr. Janus. Beginning in a very dramatic way, Mr. Beeman stated, "If information I have just received is correct, you will find the bones of the Peking man in the Nationalist Chinese Museum on Taiwan, along with other Chinese treasures which the Nationalists took with them when they evacuated the mainland. The bones will probably be in the original box."

When I read this, I recalled what was well known in Chinese art and archaeological circles, that hundreds of boxes containing famous masterpieces of Chinese pottery, carvings, paintings and the treasures excavated at An-yang had been sent off to Taiwan just before the Communists had taken Peking. But that the Peking fossils were among these was a totally new version of the fate of these relics.

Mr. Beeman, in his letter, continued:

I came about this information in a rather strange way . . .
at a cocktail party given by a Japanese officer who was
about to return to Japan after serving three years as
liaison officer at the Wright Patterson Air Force Base in
Dayton. This is the same fellow through whom I tried to

obtain information on the Japanese soldiers who participated in the capture of Camp Holcomb in Chingwangtao.

Among the guests at the cocktail party was a
Chinese Nationalist officer who is also serving as a
liaison officer at Wright Patterson AFB. His name is
Colonel Weh (Wei Ta-nien) and he has been in the
Nationalist Air Force for about thirty years. He has
served three tours of duty in this country, including his
initial training during the early part of World War II.

I naturally struck up a conversation with him and in
the course of conversation I indicated that I was involved in the search for Peking man. I asked if he knew
what I meant by Peking man. He stated that he did, that
he had read that a Chinese Nationalist general had
brought a box of bones, which he had not opened, with
him from North China and that they were probably
stored along with other items from the mainland in the
Nationalist Museum.

The whole thing, to me, is quite plausible since the
Japanese must have recognized that the only means of
disposal of items looted at Chingwangtao was through
the Chinese. Also, the only Chinese in a position to buy
them, of course, were the wealthier Chinese, who were
for the most part Nationalist in political philosophy.
Furthermore, just as the bones originally were given to
the military—the Marines—for removal from China in
1940 [actually 1941], so they might also logically have
been given to the military—the Nationalist Army—for
removal from the mainland in 1947.

You will recall that the Chinese Nationalists have
been very reluctant to display the treasures removed
from the mainland, probably out of fear that they might
be stolen since they are well aware of the fact that the
Chinese Communists would like to have the treasures
returned.

This protectionist attitude on the part of the Nationalists could very well account for the mystery of the
Peking man.

The nature of the packing, I feel certain, would preclude destruction of the bones. They must be in existence somewhere and, in the light of my conversation with Colonel Weh, I am hopeful that they will be found in the Nationalist Museum and in good condition.

If such is the case, it will no doubt require considerable international persuasion to cause them to be made available to the scientific world and negate any chance that the bones might be returned to Peking.

Where do we go from here? Could Dr. Shapiro convince them to make the bones available for study with modern-day techniques? How do we get them to tell us whether or not they actually do possess the bones?

This letter and a following one annotating and footnoting its predecessor had naturally enough fired Mr. Janus' zeal, and he had decided to go to Taiwan to investigate this latest lead. He told me the essence of these communications and asked for my help in establishing contact with the National Museum of History in Taiwan, the institution referred to in Mr. Beeman's letter as the Nationalist Museum.

My immediate reaction was one of extreme doubt. It was, of course, true that many Chinese treasures had been sent to Taiwan, but not until 1947. If the fossils had been recovered by that time, it would have been known to many of the deeply involved Chinese scholars who had remained in Peking—Pei to name one. And this knowledge would have been disseminated around the world.

Moreover, several years ago I had received a request from Dr. Pao, who was then the director of the museum, for a copy of one of the casts of Peking man that we had at The American Museum of Natural History. He needed this for an exhibit he was then planning. I had granted his request with pleasure and had received a very grateful acknowledgement. Obviously, if the original were stored in his own museum, it is unlikely that he would have made such a request of me. For these reasons in particular, I expressed my doubts to Mr. Janus, but I agreed to write on his behalf.

A couple of weeks later, I received a postcard from Taiwan in which Mr. Janus thanked me for my letter of introduction and reported a warm reception, but, as I suspected, he found no trace of Peking man having found lodging at the National Museum of History. Shortly thereafter, I received a letter from Dr. Ho Hao-tien, the present director of the museum, enclosing clips from the *China News* and the *China Post*. Both these newspapers printed stories of Mr. Janus' visit and his search for the fossils, and reported that he had raised his reward to $150,000 for information leading to the recovery of the fossils. They also referred to still another lead that Mr. Janus was exploring. This came from a Russian-American named "Petroff Alexis" (Alexis Petroff?), who had taught biology in Shanghai from 1938 to 1945. He was alleged to have told Janus that the fossils were sent to Yalta in the Crimea aboard a Russian ship. The newspapers reported that Mr. Janus had assigned a representative of The Greek Heritage Foundation in Yalta to investigate the claim.

One of the extraordinary things about this whole affair is the proliferation of stories about the fate of the fossils. In addition to those I have outlined in some detail, there are a series of variations on the versions I have described as well as a number of obvious fantasies. Mr. Janus was reported by the Taiwan press as having met with some 400 persons in connection with his search and discovering 395 leads. None of them, he is reported as saying, got him anywhere. A good deal of this can of course be attributed to the reward that was offered for information. Easy money is always a stimulating factor, and no doubt many of the correspondents who wrote to Mr. Janus were influenced by this. Then, too, there are a not inconsiderable number who compulsively respond to such an appeal, their imaginations running riot or overwhelmed by the conviction of a special insight. The publicity given to the story most probably also played a role. But even allowing for all this, what emerges is a far wider knowledge of the existence of these fossils than I would have assumed, and a far greater awareness of the tragedy of their disappearance or loss.

The variations and inconsistencies in the accounts by individuals who were most closely involved in the events is also puzzling. Time, of course, has a way of distorting the past. And the human ego also plays tricks.

Certain events seem clearly established. There can be little doubt that the fossils were, in fact, packed and prepared for shipment to the United States by the Chinese and American officials of the Peking Union Medical College and the Cenozoic Research Laboratory. The records and witnesses for this are abundant and clear. It is also well authenticated that at least two boxes containing these relics were delivered to the Marine Corps in Peking for transferral by train to Camp Holcomb in Tientsin, where they were to await the S.S. *President Harrison* for shipment to the United States.

That these boxes reached Camp Holcomb is also confirmed by reliable sources. But from this point, the conflicting testimony increases. I am inclined to discount Colonel Ashurst's conclusion that the boxes were seized on the train at Camp Holcomb and rifled by Japanese soldiers. Communication between headquarters in Peking and the contingent at Camp Holcomb, both under arrest and clearly unable to exchange information, would have been virtually cut off. And Colonel Ashurst's reconstruction of the events at the camp might well have been based on news filtering through various sources. I see no reason to question Mr. Davis' account, that the boxes were removed from the train before the Japanese appeared and had been stored in his own room.

From here on, one's imagination and guesswork take over. Is there any proof, for example, that the boxes that Dr. Foley received had not previously been ransacked? Dr. Foley declared that he himself had never opened them, and that they appeared to have been undisturbed. What happened to the box that was treasured through three prison camps? Is it possible that the boxes stored in Tientsin still survive with their contents? Can one altogether dismiss the possibility that one of the more knowledgeable Marines gathered up fossils that were discarded by Japanese looking for treasures in the boxes and, in their ignorance, casting aside a form of jewel of a value beyond their comprehension? Will the anonymous lady ever reappear so that her "war booty" can be authenticated?

At the moment, these and numerous similar questions can only go unanswered. There is no easy solution. Although some authorities have resigned themselves to the complete and irretrievable loss of the fossils, somehow this last possibility strikes me as the most devastating of all. If they had been stolen or hidden away, one might continue to hope that sometime—somewhere—somehow they might reappear and once again occupy the niche that such treasures deserve. But their being swept away into a rubbish heap has the horror and sadness that, for example, would overwhelm one on hearing that Shakespeare's original manuscripts had been miraculously discovered and then burned by a maid as worthless old papers.

I find this a tragic end that I am not yet prepared to accept until every clue has been explored and pursued. I would hope that an international group or committee, co-operating fully with the Chinese, might be established to carry out such a responsible investigation. At this stage, however, we can only speculate while we mourn.

GEOLOGICAL TIME SCALE

GEOLOGICAL ERAS	GEOLOGICAL EPOCHS	GLACIAL PERIODS	BEGAN YEARS AGO
	Holocene (recent)		9–12 thousand
	Pleistocene	Würm, Riss, Mindel, Günz	2 million
Cenozoic	Pliocene		7 million
	Miocene		24 million
	Oligocene		37 million
	Eocene		54 million
	Paleocene		65 million
Mesozoic	Cretaceous		136 million
	Jurassic		190–195 million
	Triassic		225 million
Paleozoic	Permian		280 million
	Carboniferous		345 million
	Devonian		395 million
	Silurian		430–440 million
	Ordovician		500 million
	Cambrian		570 million
Precambrian			5? billion

Geological dating in absolute numbers of years is still a somewhat controversial matter. The figures given above represent current conservative estimates by specialists.

CHART OF MAN'S EVOLUTION

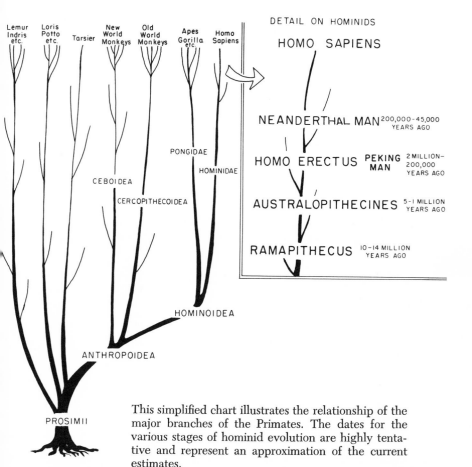

DETAIL ON HOMINIDS

Lemur Indris etc. | Loris Potto etc. | Tarsier | New World Monkeys | Old World Monkeys | Apes Gorilla etc. | Homo Sapiens

HOMO SAPIENS

NEANDERTHAL MAN 200,000-45,000 YEARS AGO

PONGIDAE

HOMINIDAE

HOMO ERECTUS PEKING MAN 2 MILLION– 200,000 YEARS AGO

CEBOIDEA

CERCOPITHECOIDEA

AUSTRALOPITHECINES 5-1 MILLION YEARS AGO

RAMAPITHECUS 10-14 MILLION YEARS AGO

HOMINOIDEA

ANTHROPOIDEA

PROSIMII

This simplified chart illustrates the relationship of the major branches of the Primates. The dates for the various stages of hominid evolution are highly tentative and represent an approximation of the current estimates.

INDEX